THE STANLEY BOOK OF
WOODWORKING
TOOLS, TECHNIQUES
AND PROJECTS

THE STANLEY BOOK OF
WOODWORKING
TOOLS, TECHNIQUES
AND PROJECTS

MARK FINNEY

BETTERWAY BOOKS
CINCINNATI, OHIO

First published in 1994 by
B.T. Batsford Ltd
4 Fitzhardinge Street
London W1H 0AH

First published in North America
in 1994 by
Betterway Books
An imprint of F&W Publications
1507 Dana Avenue
Cincinnati, Ohio 45207

© Mark Finney 1994
Furniture designs and working drawings © Mark Finney 1994
Illustrations © Sandra Pond and Will Giles 1994
Photographs © Stanley Tools
Photography by Latent Image, Sheffield 1994

Commissioning Editor: Samantha Stead
Designer: Janet James
Assistant Editor: Abigail Glover
Production Manager: Peter Colley

Typeset by Servis Filmsetting Ltd, Manchester
and printed in Germany

ISBN 1 55870 379 9

CONTENTS

ACKNOWLEDGEMENTS

This book is dedicated to the dozens of woodworkers I meet every year who, through their patience and sheer hard work, succeed in making some truly outstanding pieces of furniture. I hope this manual will help to improve their skills as well as encourage the newcomer to the craft of woodworking.

The book would not have been possible without the help and backup of a dedicated team. Special thanks go to Kim Cave and Samantha Stead for getting the project going in the first place and particularly in the case of Samantha, for the endless hours on the phone getting things right.

I am grateful also to Abigail Glover of B.T. Batsford for the constant support, and to Gordon Warr and John Kelsey for all their help and advice. Thanks are due to the illustrators, Sandra Pond and Will Giles (and even Sandra's father on occasion). Particular thanks go to Janet James who, as the designer, really got to grips with what was needed and has done a superb job.

Thanks also to the rest of the team – Graham Connell for his help with the projects, Dave and Richard at Lavers for the timber samples, and All Tools and Heeley Tool Company of Sheffield for the loan of some of the tools. I am grateful especially to Mike Stenton of Stanley Tools for collecting an assortment of 'objects' and organising the photography.

Finally, a very special thank you to Sue, my wife, for all her hard work, enthusiasm and constant encouragement from start to finish.

Thanks again everyone.

MARK FINNEY

FOREWORD

There is little more truly satisfying than taking a piece of raw wood and transforming it into a beautiful, functional piece of furniture. Working with fine quality hand tools, and learning to use them to make the most of wood's natural strength and enhance its beauty, makes for particularly rewarding woodworking.

We at STANLEY have been producing the finest quality hand tools for over 150 years. Starting from modest beginnings in America, we have developed over the last century and a half into the world's leading hand tools manufacturer. Our basic philosophy has been the driving and sustaining force throughout: to us, quality and integrity are essential in all things. Phenomenal effort goes into developing and testing every single tool we make to ensure its quality, precision and suitability for the job.

We live in an age where, in almost all walks of life, modern machine methods are taking over from traditional hand techniques. Power tools and machines in woodworking certainly give good results, but there will always be a place for hand skills, and by taking the time to learn how to use the tools to their best effect, you will give yourself an excellent basis for all kinds of woodworking.

As one of the world's best tool companies, we are proud to have joined with one of the world's best woodworking publishers to produce a book that is packed with information, is presented in a lively, friendly and easy-to-use design, and really teaches you all you need either to start woodworking from scratch, or to improve your basic skills. Even if you have never picked up a chisel in your life, by the time you reach the end of this book you will be able to make six pieces of furniture ranging from basic to more advanced – and, what's more important, you should have had a good deal of pleasure on the way.

Enjoy your woodworking!

STANLEY TOOLS

CONVERSION CHART

Depending on where you are in the world you may be used to metric or U.S. measurements, or both. This chart gives you exact conversions for reference, though bear in mind that in practice, and throughout the text of this book, very small degrees of measurement are usually rounded up or down – so, for example, the equivalent to a ¼in drill bit appears as 6mm, as it is sold, not 6.35mm, which is the exact conversion. However, there will be occasions when an exact conversion is desirable.

in	mm	in	mm	in	mm	in	mm
1/64	0.40	1/2	12.70	1	25.4	33	838.2
1/32	0.79	33/64	13.10	2	50.8	34	863.6
3/64	1.19	17/32	13.49	3	76.2	35	889
1/16	1.59	35/64	13.89	4	101.6	36	914.4
5/64	1.98	9/16	14.29	5	127	37	939.8
3/32	2.38	37/64	14.68	6	152.4	38	965.2
7/64	2.78	19/32	15.08	7	177.8	39	990.6
1/8	3.18	39/64	15.48	8	203.2	40	101.6
9/64	3.57	5/8	15.88	9	228.6	41	1041.4
5/32	3.97	41/64	16.27	10	254	42	1066.8
11/64	4.37	21/32	16.67	11	279.4	43	1092.2
3/16	4.76	43/64	17.07	12	304.8	44	1117.6
13/64	5.16	11/16	17.46	13	330.2	45	1143
7/32	5.56	45/64	17.86	14	355.6	46	1168.4
15/64	5.95	23/32	18.26	15	381	47	1193.8
1/4	6.35	47/64	18.65	16	406.4	48	1219.2
17/64	6.75	3/4	19.05	17	431.8	49	1244.6
9/32	7.14	49/64	19.45	18	457.2	50	1270
19/64	7.54	25/32	19.88	19	482.6	51	1295.4
5/16	7.94	51/64	20.24	20	508	52	1320.8
21/64	8.33	13/16	20.64	21	533.4	53	1346.2
11/32	8.73	53/64	21.03	22	558.8	54	1371.6
23/64	9.13	27/32	21.43	23	584.2	55	1397
3/8	9.53	55/64	21.83	24	609.6	56	1422.4
25/64	9.92	7/8	22/23	25	635	57	1447.8
13/32	10.32	57/64	22.62	26	660.4	58	1473.2
27/64	10.72	29/32	23.02	27	685.8	59	1498.6
7/16	11.11	59/64	23.42	28	711.2	60	1524
29/64	11.51	15/16	23.81	29	736.6	61	1549.4
15/32	11.91	61/64	24.21	30	762	62	1574.8
31/64	12.30	31/32	24.61	31	787.4	63	1600.2
		63/64	25.00	32	812.8		

HOW TO USE THIS BOOK

In a world where there seems to be a machine that will do just about anything, do hand tools for woodworking still have an important role to play? The answer is a resounding yes! Tried and tested techniques, perfected generations ago, are still used today and will continue to be used for many years to come.

Traditional hand tools are efficient and simple shapers of wood, guaranteeing accuracy every time, if they are used properly.

The aim of this book is to show you the tools that build up a tool kit and to explain how to use them; to take you through the techniques for preparing wood, laying out and cutting joints, assembling furniture and finishing. At the back of the book there are projects that have been specially designed to put into practice some of the skills you have learned.

In woodworking there are often several, equally valid, ways of doing things, and experienced woodworkers will always have their own favorite methods. If anyone tells you that there is another way than the one described in this book, then all to the good – if woodworking is to survive and develop then the sharing and passing on of ideas and knowledge is crucial. What I can guarantee is that all the techniques explained in this book are tried and trusted – and if you follow these instructions you will enjoy safe and satisfying woodworking.

As you go through this book you will find basic instructions for woodworking, and all sorts of tips, advice, technical talk boxes and shopping guides. At the beginning of each section you will find a practical explanation of things contained within it and there are some general points too, that are appropriate for the whole book.

OLD TOOLS

In the Tools section of this book you will find shopping guides which will tell you what it is essential to buy if you are building up your tool kit from scratch. You may already have an old set of tools handed on to you by a father or grandfather, or one you had at school, or just a collection pulled together from fleamarkets and yard sales. Do remember that all hand tools, especially old ones, must be suitable for the job for which you are going to use them. Just because a tool is old, it does not necessarily mean that it is better quality or will perform better. Always make a point of checking the soles of planes for flatness, layout equipment for accuracy, and ensure your saw blades are sharp and straight.

RIGHT AND LEFT-HANDED WOODWORKERS

For the sake of simplicity and space, the instructions in this book for holding tools and for woodworking techniques assume that the woodworker is right-handed. If you are left-handed, you do not need special left-handed tools – simply reverse the hands described in the instructions accordingly.

PRACTICING

If you are unsure of a technique, use scrap pieces of wood to practice on first. If you are to practice successfully, it is vital that you take proper time and care to prepare the wood correctly, even if it is to be thrown away afterward. If you are practicing finishing it is especially important to make sure that the wood samples are planed and sanded to the same standard as a finished project.

GETTING STARTED

First you need enthusiasm, followed by time, patience and a willingness to
make mistakes and learn from them.

THE WORKSHOP

Your workplace might be anything
from a corner of a garage to a fully
equipped workshop. If you have a
choice, look for somewhere with a
good daylight source and with good
ventilation. An even more important
thing to consider is the dryness (or
wetness) of the workplace, as this will
affect the stability of the wood itself.

WORKSHOP EQUIPMENT

You should always work on a flat,
undamaged surface, and so the first
essential is a well-made workbench,
preferably with a vise (see page 54).
The first project in this book, on page
104, is a good, simple workbench
design (shown below).

Coveralls or a woodworker's apron
will protect your clothes from dust,
glue and spillages – those with a large
pocket in the front for holding pencils
and tape measures are particularly
useful, but do not keep sharp knives or
chisels in them. It could be very dangerous if you bend down.

A dust cover, or old sheet, is useful
for covering up other pieces of work,
especially if they have been finished,
when you are sanding or machining.

UNDERSTANDING THE MATERIALS

MOISTURE IN WOOD

Wood is hygroscopic, which means that as a material, it will either absorb or lose moisture to the damper or dryer atmosphere that surrounds it. This may take a few hours or several days to happen, but if it does, the wood will expand as it becomes wetter or shrink as it dries – witness the door that sticks in wet weather.

For woodworkers, most problems with moisture in wood occur as you move it from one place to another, for example from an outdoor workshop into your living room, or straight from the lumber yard to near a hot radiator. In extreme cases this may result in warping, cracks and splits. It makes no difference how long a tree has been felled, as the wood will always try to recondition itself to its new environment. So, for example, an older piece of furniture stored outdoors will absorb moisture from the air, resulting in each component slowly expanding, perhaps even pulling the joints apart as it does so.

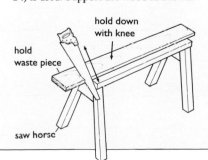

wood **+** water (moisture) **=** expansion

OR

wood **+** heat **=** contraction

Wood is hygroscopic:
it expands or contracts as it gains or loses moisture

HOW TO LOOK AFTER WOOD

Let us assume you have bought dry wood from a lumber yard. If you work on it for a few days in a workshop that is damp, the wood will expand in the workshop and then contract again later when the wood is brought indoors to a dryer environment. It is wise, therefore, to keep wood in surroundings as similar as possible to where it will be finally placed, taking pieces to the workshop only when they are needed. When you have finished working on them, bring them back to their dryer environment – even accidentally leaving the wood in a damp workshop overnight can cause it to swell slightly and possibly distort. If your workshop is dry, of course, or is about the same moisture content as indoors, there should not be a problem and you can store the wood there safely.

> **IMPORTANT**
> Make sure you do not confuse coldness in a workshop with dampness.

Before starting a project you may need to cut long lengths of wood or sheet materials down to more manageable sizes.

CROSSCUTTING

Solid wood may need cutting to length (crosscutting) ready for work to commence. Here a crosscut saw (see page 24) is used. Support the wood as shown.

It is important to provide support to the wood (including the waste) for both safety and to prevent damage.

RIPPING BOARDS ALONG THEIR LENGTH

If you are to rip the wood along its length, a slightly longer saw is more appropriate but it must be capable of sawing along the grain (see page 25).

hold down with knee

hold waste piece

saw horse

Ripping boards along their length. Support using two saw horses

> **NOTE** Sheet materials should be held on two saw horses, making sure that the waste is properly supported so that it does not flap during sawing. Very thin sheets can be laid on two planks, placed across both saw horses on either side and parallel to the intended saw cut. When cutting sheet materials, stop them from moving around by using your knee if necessary and use a relaxed stroke to saw along a marked line. If the saw binds in the saw cut, try using a little candle wax to lubricate the blade, and gently wedge open the kerf (saw cut) with a small wedge to give the saw more clearance (see also page 125).

SECONDARY CONDITIONING

Before using newly purchased wood it is preferable to secondary condition, particularly if you are to use it for important joinery or furniture. Secondary conditioning will help to stabilize the wood. This is necessary because the moisture content of new wood is generally higher than that of, say, a centrally heated room, and to avoid problems occuring later on, you should, ideally, try to make one match the other.

HOW TO SECONDARY CONDITION WOOD

There are several important points to remember which will help to keep the boards flat and stable.

• Store the wood in an environment similar to that where you will put the finished furniture.
• Keep the wood flat, never propped upright. Keep the bottom planks off the ground with chocks and stack the wood level as shown.
• Remember that whether it has been air-dried or kiln-dried at the lumber yard, solid wood should still be secondary conditioned before use.
• If you cut the wood to the approximate sizes needed before secondary conditioning, the entire process will be speeded up and will also make handling the wood easier.
• Use pieces of wood of equal thickness for the stickers. These are used to separate the wood, providing ventilation helping it to dry out. Place stickers between the planks and directly in line on top of each other. The stickers should never be further apart than 15in (380mm) or the boards may sag.
• Put weights on the top boards over a row of stickers to keep them flat.
• Secondary conditioning will take around two to three weeks for 1in (25mm) thick softwood and three to four weeks for 1in (25mm) thick hardwood at an average room temperature – longer for thicker planks.

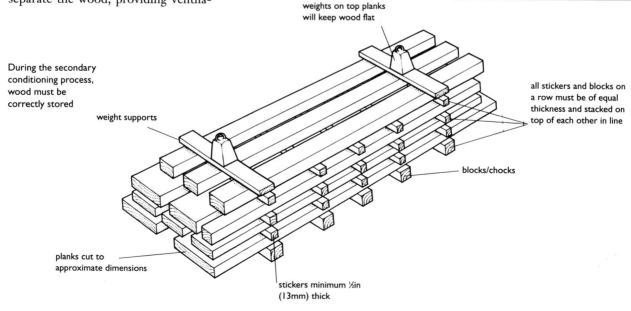

weights on top planks will keep wood flat

During the secondary conditioning process, wood must be correctly stored

weight supports

all stickers and blocks on a row must be of equal thickness and stacked on top of each other in line

blocks/chocks

planks cut to approximate dimensions

stickers minimum ½in (13mm) thick

SAFETY IN THE WORKSHOP

With traditional hand tools and skills, there may well be more likelihood of you damaging the wood than yourself. However, accidents can happen and you must take precautions to avoid injury. Look after your fingers and eyes in particular, and always have a first aid box at hand.

1 Woodworker's apron with pouch   2 Safety gloves   3 Ear protectors
4 Safety goggles   5 Dust mask   6 Dust respirator

GOLDEN RULES

- When using sharp hand tools, such as chisels, always push the blade away from you, so that if you slip you will not cut yourself.
- Never wear jewelry or loose-fitting clothes. Tie back your hair if necessary when in the workshop.
- Wear suitable ear, nose and eye protection when appropriate.
- When finishing, always open a window for ventilation. Some materials commonly used in woodworking give off strong odors or are highly flammable.
- Always store stains and finishes safely and away from children.
- If at any time when you are using a tool, you do not feel in complete control, always stop! If you are using a tool correctly it should feel comfortable, so re-read the instructions and try again.

THE MATERIALS

One of the real joys of working in wood is that wood is a living material,
a renewable resource, and since every tree is different, so is every piece of wood.

HARDWOODS AND SOFTWOODS

There are over 35,000 species of hardwoods and around 200 species of softwoods throughout the world. Most of these are not suitable for general woodwork: some trees are far too small or too sparse to produce recognizable commercial timbers. Where several timbers are similar to each other they may be grouped together for sale as a mixed species. The mahogany substitutes (such as lauan) fall into this category and this accounts for the wide range of shades within a single batch of wood. The timbers listed are some of the most popular among woodworkers: all are readily available.

What is the difference between hardwoods and softwoods? Although in the majority of cases hardwoods are actually harder and tougher than softwoods, the real difference between the two is that in general, softwoods originate from cone-bearing trees and hardwoods from trees that have their seeds contained in a seed-case (so an apple tree would therefore be classified as a hardwood).

Hardwoods can in actual fact vary from being very hard (greenheart, for example, is particularly dense and tough) to extremely soft (obeche and balsa wood are both hardwoods). Some hardwoods are so heavy that they are unable to float in water. Softwoods, meanwhile, are not necessarily soft – parana pine from South America is actually harder and tougher than many hardwoods.

A good guide to the strength of each wood is its specific gravity, which compares its density to that of water, whose specific gravity is 1. Generally, the higher this figure is, the tougher and harder the wood.

GOOD ADVICE

Trees yield wood of varying qualities which are then graded. Always ask the advice of a good wood dealer when deciding which grade of wood you should select for your project. Any wood to be used for quality work should have been suitably dried before purchase.

Although a wide range of different woods is available, staining increases the choice of colors even further (see page 100 for how to apply wood stains)

TIP

Wood is often sold with the bark still on it. This is known as a waney edged board. Although prices may seem cheaper, don't forget that there will be considerably more waste. (See page 23 for converting waney edged boards.)

SOFTWOODS

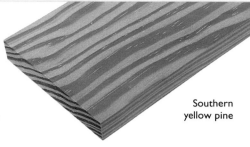

Southern
yellow pine

DOUGLAS FIR: *Pseudotsuga menziesii* – specific gravity, 0.48. From Pacific Northwest.

Light brown with reddish tone. Very distinct and bold figure, and therefore very attractive. Often overlooked as a furniture wood, but the better grades are suitable for top quality work, with the lower grades used for construction and plywood. May surface check (see page 93) while being dried.

EASTERN WHITE PINE: *Pinus strobus* – specific gravity 0.35. From eastern North America.

Very stable softwood often used for detailed moldings, patterns, and high-quality millwork. It is an easily workable, fine textured timber. Can be used for model making and carving.

REDWOOD: *Sequoia sempervirens* – specific gravity 0.37. From California and Oregon.

Extremely stable and rot-resistant wood, deep red-brown in color. Redwood is prized for interior and exterior trim. Old-growth redwood, characterized by fine, close growth rings, is now rare.

SOUTHERN YELLOW PINE: *Pinus* spp – specific gravity 0.48 to 0.59. From the Southeastern and South-Central states.

Four species – slash, shortleaf, loblolly and longleaf – constitute 90% of the mixed group of pines known as "southern yellow." They are all yellow to light brown in color, hard and relatively dense, with a strong figure. The best grades can be used for furniture but most goes to flooring, construction and pallets.

SPRUCE: *Picea spp.* – specific gravity 0.40. Sitka and Engelmann spruce come from the Pacific Northwest and Alaska; Eastern spruce is from Maine and Quebec.

The wood is soft, light and strong, colored from creamy white to pale brown. Boatbuilders and musical instrument makers prize spruce because of its light stiffness.

WESTERN WHITE PINE: *Pinus monticola* – specific gravity 0.38. From Northwest and Mountain states.

White to yellow-brown softwood, mild and workable, and widely used for furniture and interior trim. Some grades, with plentiful red knots, are sold as 'knotty pine.'

HARDWOODS

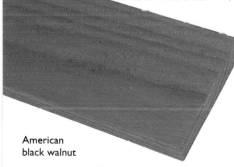

American
black walnut

ASH, WHITE: *Fraxinus americana* – specific gravity 0.60. Grows widely in Eastern and Central North America.

Ash is white to pale brown, an attractive, open-textured, ring-porous wood that works, stains and finishes well. It is used for furniture or components that need to be tough, such as tool handles. Because ash can be steam-bent and laminated, it is often used for tennis rackets and other sports equipment.

CHERRY, BLACK or PENNSYLVANIA: *Prunus serotina* – specific gravity 0.50. From Mid-Atlantic and Midwestern states.

Heartwood darkens rapidly on exposure to sunlight to an attractive pinkish brown. Superb, fine-looking wood used for furniture, cabinet and decorative work. Very close-textured and uniform, and finishes beautifully. Quartersawn cherry reveals striking ray flecks.

MAHOGANY, BRAZILIAN: *Swietenia macrophylla* – specific gravity 0.58. From Central and South America.

Pale red/brown wood, often with no strong or marked figure. It carves cleanly, and stains and finishes well. Stocks are often not from sustainable sources.

Mahogany substitutes include West African mahogany, dark red lauan and some species from Papua New Guinea. True mahogany is expensive, so any wood that has a similar grain, figure and colour, is often in demand as an alternative. Most often used for interior joinery, furniture, doors and windows.

MAPLE, SUGAR or HARD: *Acer saccharum* – specific gravity 0.57 to 0.63. From New England, Mid-Atlantic and Midwestern states.

White, hard wood with fine grain and subtle figure. Maple can be used for furniture, flooring, workbenches and shop fixtures. It cuts and planes cleanly and takes finish well, though it can be difficult to stain.

OAK, WHITE: *Quercus alba* – specific gravity 0.68. Grows throughout North America.

White oak ranges in color from pale to mid-brown/gray. It is a tough, hard wood, with very distinct pores. When quartersawn, its large rays add flash to its figure. Traditionally used for making barrels, white oak is now a top quality furniture and cabinet making wood. Stains and finishes well. Iron in the presence of moisture will react with acids in the wood and leave black stains, so keep clamps away from wet glue, and use brass or stainless steel hardware.

POPLAR, TULIP or **YELLOW:** *Liriodendron tulipifera* – specific gravity 0.42. From Mid-Atlantic and Midwestern states.

The wide sapwood is flat and creamy white, while the heartwood varies from soft brown to green, with indistinct figure. Traditionally used as a secondary wood in furniture construction.

TEAK: *Tectona grandis* – specific gravity 0.57. From Southeast Asia.

Mid/dark-brown hardwood often with thin, darker brown markings and stripes. Not usually available from sustainable sources. Works and carves very well, though it can be oily when first cut, causing problems with some finishes. Most suitable surface protection is an oil finish. Wearing a dust mask is recommended when sanding.

WALNUT, AMERICAN BLACK: *Juglans nigra* – specific gravity 0.55. From Mid-Atlantic, Midwest and Southeast, and California.

Dark brown, almost purple heartwood, as opposed to European walnut which is a mid to dark brown color with thin black streaks. Used extensively for quality furniture and gun stocks. Both American and European walnut are very expensive and supplies are often limited.

HOW TO BUY WOOD

Lumber dealers buy rough sawn planks, and you too can buy wood in an unplaned state and machine your own. You can also have wood prepared to size for you by the sawmill or dealer.

Wood is usually sold in nominal thicknesses, i.e. the size that the mill started off with, and not the finished dimensions that you buy.

The thickness of boards and planks is generally given in quarters of an inch. Thus, 6/4 (spoken as six-quarter) refers to a board that measured an inch-and-a-half thick when rough.

Softwoods tend to be sold planed on both sides and both edges (S4S, or "Surfaced Four Sides"). A smooth softwood board that actually measures ¾in thick and 5½in wide will be described as 4/4-by-six, or one-by-six. Softwood lumber is priced by the running foot, in lengths ranging from 8ft to 16ft, in 2ft increments. If you ask the lumber yard to crosscut your material to length, expect to pay to the next 2ft increment.

Hardwoods are sold by the board foot. One board foot (bf) is the equivalent of a piece of wood 12in long, 12in wide, and 1in thick. Hardwoods are sold rough, or else planed on both sides but not edge-straightened (S2S). If you dress your own wood, you can usually net ⅞in of thickness from a 4/4 hardwood board. If the mill runs it through their planer, you'll get only ¾in.

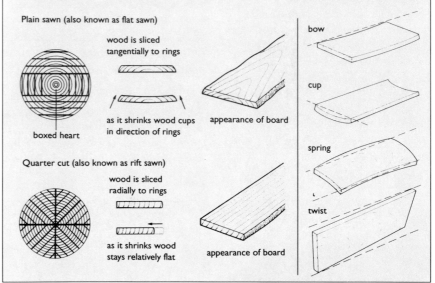

HOW WOOD CAN MOVE WHEN CUT

Plain sawn (also known as flat sawn)

wood is sliced tangentially to rings

boxed heart

as it shrinks wood cups in direction of rings

appearance of board

Quarter cut (also known as rift sawn)

wood is sliced radially to rings

as it shrinks wood stays relatively flat

appearance of board

HOW WOOD WARPS

bow

cup

spring

twist

TECHNICAL TALK

BALANCED CONSTRUCTION When one material, for example a veneer, is glued to a baseboard, unless a similar veneer is fastened to the underside too to balance it, the sheet material will cup in a similar way to solid wood.

CUP A form of warping (see above).

DEAD KNOTS Knots created when branches have been broken off a living tree and wood has grown around them. The dark line around their outside edges is old bark.

LIVE KNOTS Knots created by branches that were active when the tree was felled.

GRADING Batches of timber divided according to quality.

HOMOGENOUS A material of uniform particle size and construction throughout.

NOMINAL SIZES The wood sizes with which a sawmill starts before planing: these can vary. Remember that if the sawmill has resawn the wood, the nominal size itself may be smaller than expected.

RING-POROUS Describes hardwoods that have a very definite pattern created by the alternating coarse and fine texture of each ring, e.g. elm, oak and ash.

WOOD TYPES

SOFTWOODS

1 Douglas fir
2 Eastern white pine
3 Western red cedar

HARDWOODS

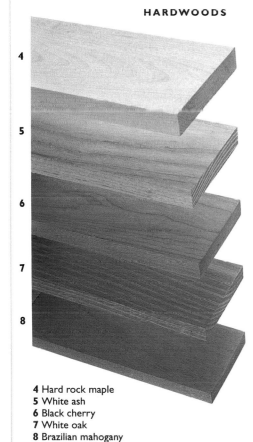

4 Hard rock maple
5 White ash
6 Black cherry
7 White oak
8 Brazilian mahogany

MAN-MADE BOARDS

There is nothing quite like real wood, but if expense is a factor, or where there may be problems with the movement of solid wood (see page 11) you may prefer to use man-made sheet materials.

These fall into several categories.

BLOCKBOARD AND LAMINBOARD: Manufactured boards consisting of a thick core of wooden strips held in place by veneers glued to each face. Laminboard has much thinner strips in the core and although similar to blockboard, is much more stable. Suitable for internal use only. Not suitable for areas which may become wet, such as near sinks and baths.

CHIPBOARD: Essentially a compressed mulch of wood chips and glue, which, after being left to dry, cut to size and sanded, produces a relatively cheap sheet material. The quality of chipboard can vary tremendously depending on the size of chips used, especially in the core of the board. Suitable for internal use only. Often available with colored or decorative patterned plastic laminate on both sides. Extensively used for knock-down furniture, kitchens, fitted furniture and, depending on the density, floors and general joinery.

FIBERBOARD: Not to be confused with MDF, true fiberboard has natural wood fibers (not wood chips) and resins compressed to thickness to make a sheet material. There are three kinds: soft board, used for insulation materials and suspended ceiling tiles; medium board, used for notice boards; and hardboard. Hardboard is a very familiar sheet material. Although most commonly it has a shiny, dark-brown face, it is also available with patterns or decoration impressed into it. Before using hardboard, soak the back first with

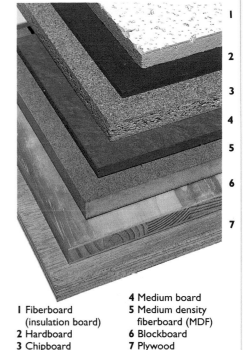

1 Fiberboard (insulation board)
2 Hardboard
3 Chipboard
4 Medium board
5 Medium density fiberboard (MDF)
6 Blockboard
7 Plywood

water and leave it to dry, to allow it to condition and stabilize to a new environment. Always store flat.

MEDIUM DENSITY FIBERBOARD (MDF): A fine homogenous board consisting of fine wood fibers held together by the use of adhesives. MDF is relatively expensive but as a material it will take veneers, is easily molded, takes stains and finishes and, unlike chipboard, satisfactorily holds wood screws. MDF is a quite different sheet material, and a very welcome recent addition to the others described above. It produces irritating dust when worked and suitable precautions should be taken.

PLYWOOD: Manufactured from thin veneers of wood, cross-laminated for extra strength. Plywood usually has an odd number of layers to create a balanced construction. If an even number of veneers is used, there is an increased chance of the board twisting. Plywood is available with decorative veneers bonded to one or both faces and some types are used for external as well as internal work depending on the type of glue used. Marine plywood is the most durable external plywood.

Tools

Tools can be expensive, so it is very important to buy right. Always select each tool as you need it rather than all at once and buy the best you can afford. This way you will build up your tool kit slowly and carefully, adding to it as you get more advanced.

On the following pages, each section is carefully laid out and explains what tools do and how they work, what to look for and what questions to ask. There are shopping guides to help you decide what you need as well as tips and technical talk boxes which cut through the jargon.

If you have a specialist interest, there are many more tools to be found in the full Stanley Tools Catalog.

MEASURING AND LAYOUT TOOLS

The whole point of woodworking is to produce straight lengths of wood, to make true and accurate frames and carcases, and to position and fit doors, drawers and shelves. It stands to reason that the instruments you use to do the layout should be as precise as possible.

The more accurate the tools you use, the better the chances are of your workmanship looking professional. Always take extra time and care to work exactly to any markings you have made. You should never be tempted in quality woodwork to think 'that's close enough'! In some instances you may even need to use precision engineering quality measuring and layout equipment.

It is important to work as accurately as you can because even such apparently small measurements as $\frac{1}{32} - \frac{1}{16}$in (1–2mm) can easily be seen later. If you need proof, then reach for a ruler and look at the actual size that this measures. Now, imagine a gap as large as that on one of your joints.

It can often be very tempting to bypass the careful preparation and accurate layout of wood, because of your understandable enthusiasm for wanting to get on with the woodworking itself. But the importance of preparation and layout really cannot be underestimated. Done poorly, everyone can see the joint that didn't quite make it, or the top that doesn't quite fit. But done well – that's a different story altogether.

THE KNIFE VERSUS THE PENCIL

You use a knife to lay out the exact positions of joints. It is much more accurate than a pencil and will actually cut through the fibers of the wood, allowing the saw or chisel to produce a fine, clean edge. Pencils are for marking information on wood – such as face side and face edge symbols (see page 62) – and can be used to show the approximate positions of joints in joinery work.

However, if you are actually a little unsure about using a knife (and this may be a wise practice if you are a beginner), you can, of course, use a sharp 2-H first to mark out the position of joints, and then go over any lines to be cut with the knife.

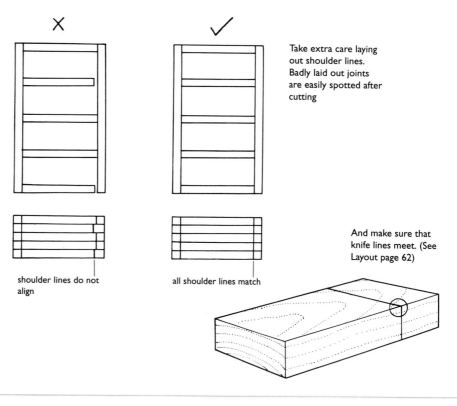

shoulder lines do not align

all shoulder lines match

Take extra care laying out shoulder lines. Badly laid out joints are easily spotted after cutting

And make sure that knife lines meet. (See Layout page 62)

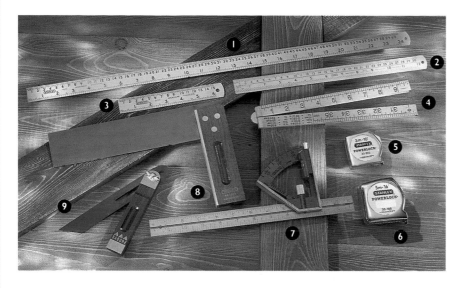

1 24in (600mm) steel rule
2 12in (300mm) steel rule
3 6in (150mm) steel rule
4 Folding rule
5 10ft (3m) steel
6 16ft (5m) steel case tape measure
7 Combination square
8 9in (225mm) try square
9 Sliding bevel

case tape measure

TAPES

A steel tape is probably the wood-worker's most basic measuring tool. It must be looked after to stop either the hook or the blade being damaged as the graduations will then be difficult to see and you will be unable to take true readings. Some tapes have a blade lock to stop the blade from springing back inside the case. This is a handy extra. Better quality tapes have much more accurate markings and a more robust casing (in some cases made from steel) which will give many years of service. A tape with a sliding hook, which moves to compensate for its thickness when measuring internal and external dimensions, is well worth having.

STEEL RULES

Steel rules are more accurate and con-venient than tape measures when working on small components, rails and panels. They are especially suit-able for measuring the distances between shoulder lines. The gradua-tions usually start right at one end of the rule, enabling it to be pushed into tight corners, and easily allowing you to take a true reading. The most popular sizes are 6in (150mm), 12in (300mm), 24in (600mm) and 39⅜in (1m) lengths. The one meter rule is also known as a meter stick. Steel rules are also very useful for checking the flatness of surfaces during hand planing (see page 66).

COMBINATION SQUARES

A combination square is a particularly useful tool. For the serious or profes-sional craftsman in fact, it really is a must. Good quality combination squares will allow you accurately to mark out right angles, bevels (see page 70), miters, as well as a wide variety of compound angles. The combination square can also double up as a try square for checking internal angles, or can be used as separate steel rules. It can even become a depth gauge simply by putting the stock on the surface of the wood and sliding the rule into the hole to check how deep it is.

FOLDING RULES

Folding rules are traditionally made from wood, although they are available in plastic and steel too. They are used for the same purposes as a steel rule but fold up to make them much more convenient to carry. For on-site work this also helps stop the rule being acci-dentally damaged.

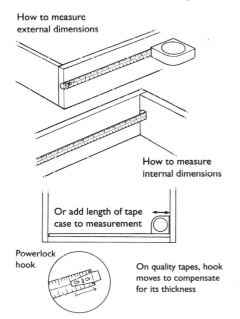

How to measure external dimensions

How to measure internal dimensions

Or add length of tape case to measurement

Powerlock hook

On quality tapes, hook moves to compensate for its thickness

TRY SQUARE

The try square is used to mark lines across the surface of wood. To use one, put the point of a pencil or knife on the wood in the correct place and then slide the square up to it. The square will automatically stop in the correct position for laying out. Hold the square firmly, pushing down on to the wood. Be careful not to slip when using a knife.

Try squares with a traditional wooden stock are used both for layout and also for checking the squareness of cabinet work and frames during gluing up (see page 84).

HOW TO TEST A SQUARE FOR BEING SQUARE

from a true edge knife a line

Turn square over to check blade against knife line. An accurate square will line up exactly

SLIDING BEVEL

A sliding bevel will allow you to set up to a specific angle and then transfer this information exactly to the workpiece. Ensure that when in use, you tighten the adjustment nut or locking lever properly, and do not drop or knock it as this will change the setting. When laying out, do not push excessively against the blade with a marking knife as this too may accidentally alter the angle.

KNIVES

Knives used for woodworking fall into two categories – layout knives, and craft and trimming knives.

Layout knives have a flattish wooden handle and, more importantly, the blade has a bevel on only one side. Use the layout knife by putting the face without the bevel against a square or a template, such as another joint – as, for example, when laying out dovetails (see page 81).

Craft knives are much sharper than layout knives and are suitable for cutting materials such as veneers, paper or card. If you use a craft knife as a layout knife you must allow for the width of the bevel on the blade. Be careful with craft knives. Always work so that if you slip, there will be no chance of serious injury.

1 Spirit level	**5** Stanley trimming knife
2 Cutting gauge	with a selection of blades
3 Marking gauge	**6** Calipers
4 Marking knife	**7** Dividers
	8 Dovetail gauge

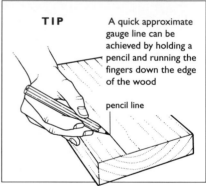

TIP A quick approximate gauge line can be achieved by holding a pencil and running the fingers down the edge of the wood

pencil line

The typical Stanley trimming knife is a particularly tough knife offering a choice of differently shaped blades. These are used where extra precision is required or where you need to work in an awkward space or very tight corner.

THE DIFFERENCE BETWEEN A LAYOUT KNIFE AND A CRAFT KNIFE

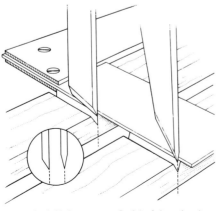

Layout knife blade is only bevelled on one side allowing it to be pushed up to a square

Craft knife has a bevel on both edges creating a "v". This must be allowed for during layout

TECHNICAL TALK

CARCASE Main part of a structure, framework of furniture.

DEPTH GAUGE Used to check the depth of a hole or rabbet.

MITER One of the simplest methods of jointing two pieces of wood. Commonly used on picture frames, panelling and beadings.

SHOULDER A square projection on one or more sides of a joint.

STOCK The main part of a tool, often used as a handle.

TRY SQUARE Also known as a square or carpenter's square. Used for accurately marking right angles.

PROFILE GAUGE Used to produce a template for marking out awkward shapes.

TRAMMEL Used to scribe large arcs or circles.

VIALS The part of a spirit level that holds the liquid.

WANEY Where the bark of a tree is still present.

MARKING AND CUTTING GAUGES

Marking gauges differ from cutting gauges in that the first has a point designed for scribing lines along the grain, whereas the second has a knife for scoring the fibers of the wood across the grain.

Marking gauges are available with either one point or two (one of which is movable), and used properly they will always give true, accurate gauge lines to work to. A single pointed marking gauge could be used to lay out the depth of half-lap joints, whereas twin-pointed ones, known as mortise gauges, are used to mark out two parallel lines, for example for mortise and tenon joints.

Cutting gauges are used where it is impractical to use a square and knife across the grain. A cutting gauge will produce a scored line exactly parallel to the end of a board or panel. It is important that the end you use to guide the stock should be true and straight, and that you ensure that the stock is pushed firmly against it to create an accurate line.

DIVIDERS

Dividers are straight-legged and look a little like a pair of compasses with two points. In woodwork, they can be used to measure the widths of the pins and tails when laying out dovetail joints, or can be used to check measurements. Callipers are different from dividers in that they have bowed legs and are used for measuring the external or internal diameters of turned work or other cylindrical objects.

DOVETAIL GAUGE

A small gauge used to mark the angles of dovetail joints. Usually available as either 1:6 or 1:8 angle of slope, the steeper angle (1:6) being more suited to softwoods, and 1:8, hardwoods. You can buy a dovetail gauge or make one yourself by cutting and filing thin sheet metal to size.

STRAIGHTENING WANEY EDGED BOARDS

Waney edged boards can be marked to produce a straight line for sawing to by using a chalk line

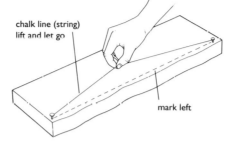

chalk line (string) lift and let go

mark left

Or you can screw or nail a straight piece of wood to the face and push that against the fence of a circular saw

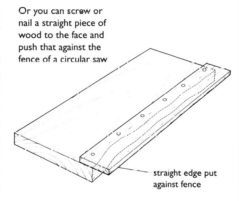

straight edge put against fence

SPIRIT LEVEL

Spirit levels are not used in traditional furniture making but are used when installing built-in furniture, including wardrobes and kitchen units. They rely on a trapped air bubble held in a liquid kept in a slightly curved, clear tube. By measuring the position of the bubble, a true horizontal or vertical surface can be found. Modern, top quality box-section spirit levels are virtually unbreakable and have sealed vials.

OTHER LAYOUT TOOLS

There are several specialist layout tools which are readily available, such as profile gauges, trammels and depth gauges. These can be used when, for example, an unusual shape or component needs to be laid out.

SAWS

Knowing how to use a saw is of fundamental importance when working in wood - but how do you know which one to choose?

TRADITIONAL SAWS

HAND SAWS

Hand saws have a flexible blade to allow you to cut through large sections of wood or across wide panels. The combination of length, toothsize and type of tooth determines the job to which each is best suited.

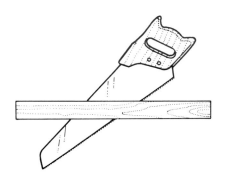

RIP SAW a long saw used to cut along the grain. Blade length 26in (650mm); TPI 4–6

CROSSCUT SAW used to cut across the grain. Blade length 24–26in (600–650mm); TPI 6–8

PANEL SAW similar to a crosscut saw but with finer teeth. Ideal for thin plywood. Blade length 20–22in (500–550mm); TPI 10–12

BACK SAWS

Back saws have a blade strengthened with either a brass or steel strip. This helps to keep the blade rigid for cutting accurate joints. Back saws are shorter than hand saws and they also have finer teeth.

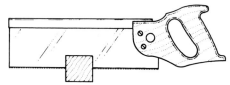

TENON SAW the most common back saw. Used to cut joints such as the mortise and tenon. Blade length 10–14in (250–350mm); TPI 12–15

DOVETAIL SAW a fine back saw designed to cut accurate joints such as the dovetail. Blade length 8in (200mm); TPI 15–22

BEAD SAW very fine back saw for cutting delicate moldings and beads. Blade length 8in (200mm); TPI 24–26

HARD POINT TEETH

Specially hardened teeth, blackened for identification, that stay sharp at least five times longer than conventional teeth. Suitable for cutting sheet materials. Not resharpenable. Disposable and generally less expensive than sharpenable saws

UPDATE

Some of these hand saws are no longer made, but you may have one in a tool box. With the introduction of new materials and manufacturing techniques, the jobs of cutting along and across the grain can now be taken care of by one hand saw, with universal teeth. These cut on the forward stroke; and they are resharpenable.

If you intend to cut sheet materials, be warned that the glue content will rapidly blunt conventional saw teeth, so choose a saw with aggressive geometry fast cut teeth. These cut on the forward and reverse strokes. Saws with these teeth include the Stanley range of Jet Cut saws.

MEASURING TOOTHSIZE

Saw teeth are measured by teeth per inch (TPI), or sometimes by points per inch (PPI). There is always one less tooth per inch than there are points per inch (e.g. 7 TPI = 8 PPI). The higher the number the finer the teeth.

QUICK GUIDE TO SIZE AND FUNCTION

Up to 7 TPI – heavy duty sawing and constructional work
8–10 TPI – general purpose sawing
11 TPI and up – fine or accurate work.

For the best results, choose the saw with the correct tooth type and size for the job you are doing.

1 Dovetail saw
2 Wooden handle universal tooth hand saw
3 Hardpoint fast cut tooth hand saw
4 Wooden handle universal tooth tenon saw
5 Hardpoint fast cut tooth tenon saw

Saw teeth cut the wood, then lift and carry out the waste in the form of sawdust. Different teeth do different jobs.

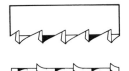

RIP SAW TEETH chisel type teeth that do not score the wood before cutting. Used along the grain only.

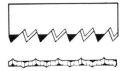

CROSSCUT TEETH knife point teeth that actually sever the fibers of the wood. Ideal for cutting across the grain.

FLEAM TEETH also known as straight or needle teeth. Designed for fast cutting across the grain. Especially suitable for softwoods.

UNIVERSAL TEETH designed to cut both along and across the grain and found on both hand and back saws.

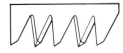

AGGRESSIVE GEOMETRY FAST CUT TEETH produce a very clean quick cut. They cut both on the back and forward strokes. Suitable for cutting modern sheet materials. These are available hardpointed for a longer life.

HOW TO USE A SAW

Always saw to an accurate line and cut on the waste side (see layout, page 62). This will help produce a good clean cut.

HOW TO USE A BACK SAW

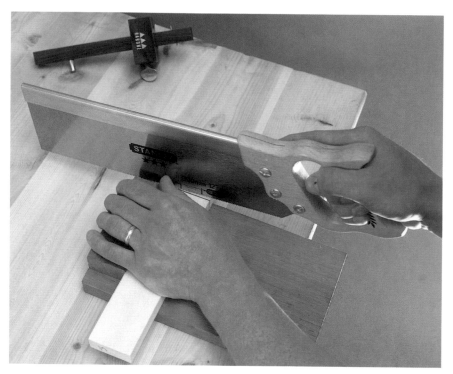

Use a bench hook and start sawing at a shallow angle. Use the thumb of your left hand as a guide

Hold the saw in your right hand and start by drawing the saw toward you lightly. Use the thumb of your other hand as a guide, resting it on the wood and up against (not underneath) the saw blade. Do not let the blade bounce or jump up and down. Now lightly push the saw away from you, and you will start to cut the wood. Use only light pressure at first, increasing it slightly as you begin to saw.

Concentrate on following the knife line and do not hold the saw too stiffly.

Relax and let the saw follow the line. Aim to saw at an angle of around 15–20 degrees to the wood (a little less when using a dovetail saw), which will allow you to cut into the top corner farthest away from you. After four or five strokes, level out and cut along the knife line on the waste side, working your way through the wood.

HANDLES AND STANCE

If you hold a saw properly, the angle of the handle should help you to stand correctly. For example, a dovetail saw handle is set low, allowing you to crouch and 'shoot' through a dovetail. On the other hand the tenon saw handle will allow you to stand more upright, so you can easily follow your layout lines.

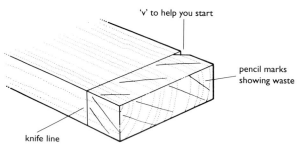

'v' to help you start

If you make a 'v' with a chisel on the waste side of the knife line, this will help the saw start in the right place

pencil marks showing waste

knife line

HOW TO USE A HAND SAW

Hand saws are not intended to be as accurate as back saws. Therefore, when cutting a sheet of plywood or a softwood joist, you can work to a clear pencil line instead of a more accurate knife line. If you make an error in layout, always clearly re-mark your work.

Sawing with a hand saw is similar to sawing with a back saw, the difference being that you start cutting at a slightly higher angle. Do not use a bench hook. Again draw back the blade using the thumb of your other hand as a guide, and the saw will begin to cut on the forward stroke. Ensure that the waste is properly supported, especially near the end of sawing. If not, as the waste falls off, the piece you want will also be damaged.

Use the full length of the saw, slightly lowering the angle after two or three strokes. Work with the entire length of your arm, using your shoulder and upper body for power and control. Relax. Let the saw do the work: do not use excessive pressure. Use a little less force at the tip, then slightly increase the pressure as you push forward, until you reach the area of blade near the handle. Draw back and push again. Simple!

TECHNICAL TALK

KERF The width of a saw cut.

SET To allow the saw blade to slide through the kerf without binding. The teeth project alternately from the side of the blade providing clearance while sawing.

BENCH HOOK Tool used to steady small sections of wood while being cut.

HANDLES Straight, pistol, closed grip and offset. There are several types of saw handle available. Pistol grips are 'open' (like a hand gun); closed grip handles are totally enclosed. Straight handles are a straight extension of the saw blade resembling the type of handle used on a file. Offset handles are usually straight handles that are cranked to one side.

SHOULDERS A square projection on one or more sides of a joint. The distance between shoulder lines creates the internal dimensions of a framework.

COPING Scribing to the exact line of a molding rather than producing a miter. The coping saw is used to create the tight curves for this work and other purposes.

SOLVING PROBLEMS

PROBLEM	CAUSE	WHAT TO DO
saw sticks in saw cut (kerf)	▶ incorrect set on saw ▶ resinous/wet wood ▶ wandering from line during cutting, thus trapping the blade	saw must be reset by a saw doctor use paraffin wax (candle wax) to lubricate blade remove blade and resaw to line
edges break out (splinter)	▶ toothsize too large for material being cut	select a finer toothed saw
wood tears out from under saw cut, especially when cutting plywood/chipboard	▶ holding saw at too steep an angle ▶ using excessive pressure	reduce angle of saw to 15–20 degrees use lighter pressure
wood tears out from underneath when cutting across the grain	▶ as above	fasten a block beneath to support the wood where the grain is tearing out, or on smaller pieces use a bench hook
saw jumps or bounces as you start sawing	▶ toothsize too large ▶ angle of sawing too steep	select a finer toothed saw reduce angle of saw

SPECIAL SAWS

Sawing isn't always about cutting joints and large pieces of wood;
there are other jobs that call for specially designed saws.

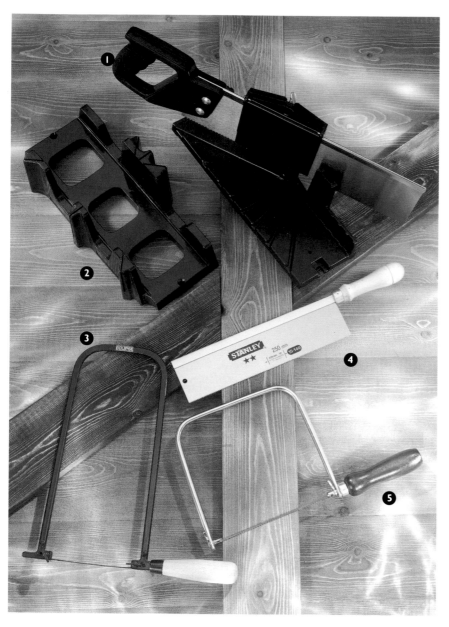

1 Saw and mitre
  guide
2 Mitre box
3 Fret saw
4 Gentleman's back
  saw
5 Coping saw

COPING AND FRET SAWS

In appearance a coping saw is similar to a fret saw, although in fact they both perform very different tasks. The coping saw is the smaller but more heavy duty of the two. It has a replaceable blade with 15–17 TPI. It is used to cut around tight curves in softwoods, most hardwoods and in man-made boards up to 1in (25mm) thick. The fret saw has a much taller, deep bowed frame and a very fine blade. Unlike a coping saw it is used to cut extremely light fretwork, and veneers.

A much larger version of the coping saw, which produces only shallow curves in thicker stock, is the traditional wooden framed bow saw. This saw is heavy and difficult to use, requiring both hands to keep control.

DISPOSABLE-BLADE JAPANESE SAWS

Several styles of Japanese saw with disposable blades have begun to appear in hardware stores and home centers. These saws come with one of two general tooth styles: thorn teeth, shaped like triangles, for ripping; and mouse teeth, very long and steep, for crosscutting. All Japanese saws are made of thin steel and cut on the pull stroke. Many people find them easier to steer than a Western saw.

Traditional Japanese saws are difficult to sharpen, but these new ones have long-lasting disposable blades made of hardened steel. The replacement blade just snaps into the plastic handle. The Japanese equivalent of a dovetail saw, called a dozuki, has about 15 TPI and is handy for trimming moldings and cutting dowel pins off flush.

HOW TO USE A COPING SAW

The coping saw can be set up to cut either on the back or on the forward stroke. (The fretsaw, on the other hand, always cuts on the back stroke.) Hold the work upright in a vise and keep the coping saw blade at right angles to the surface of the wood. As with hand and back saws, use the thumb of your left hand as a guide for the blade and use light strokes to help the saw get started. The blade is thin and brittle, so do not force it as you work or it will easily break – instead let the saw do the work. Ensure you do not allow the blade to leave the line you are following. You can help to keep control by turning the blade periodically as you cut. If the wood vibrates in the vise move it nearer to the jaws to steady it.

If you need to start cutting in a totally enclosed area, drill a small pilot hole first (preferably in a corner) and insert the coping saw blade through it, before starting to saw.

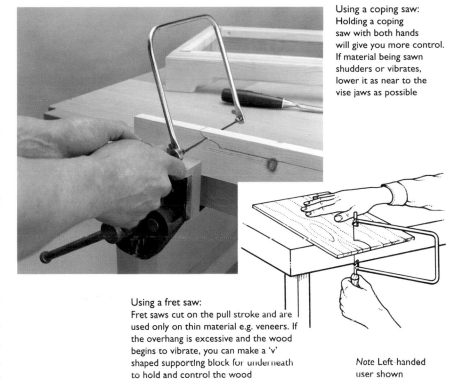

Using a coping saw: Holding a coping saw with both hands will give you more control. If material being sawn shudders or vibrates, lower it as near to the vise jaws as possible

Using a fret saw: Fret saws cut on the pull stroke and are used only on thin material e.g. veneers. If the overhang is excessive and the wood begins to vibrate, you can make a 'v' shaped supporting block for underneath to hold and control the wood

Note Left-handed user shown

TIP
When mitering lots of very small moldings or beads at 45 degrees you can use the reflection of the molding in the saw blade to give you a quick and simple guide to 90 degrees.

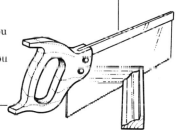

CUTTING ANGLES – THE MITER BOX

A simple miter box is a tool to allow you to cut angles at 45 degrees, useful when you need to produce a right-angled joint, for example, on panels and picture frames. It will usually cut at 90 degrees too, for cutting wood to length. More complex miter boxes can be set to cut at 30 degrees, 45 degrees, 60 degrees, 90 degrees and other angles. They can be bought complete with a back saw, which is held in place by guides. These are more expensive than the simple miter box but are able to produce very accurate joints.

PLANES

Planes are used to make wood smooth, and there are several to choose from.
Each is sharpened and set to perform different jobs.

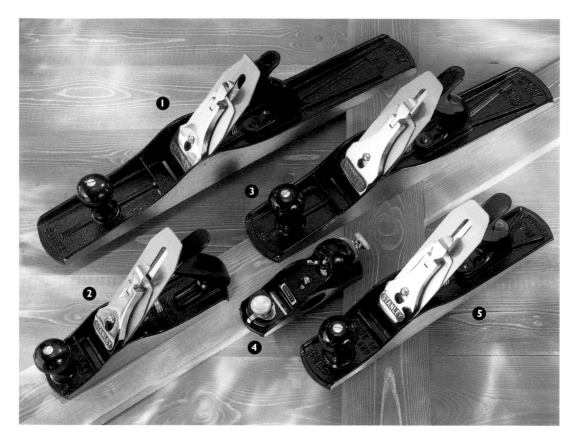

1 Jointer or try plane
2 Smoothing plane
3 Fore plane
4 Block plane
5 Jack plane

Think of a wood shaving as roughly the same thickness as a sheet of paper. Now hold just six pages of this book between your fingers and imagine a gap this wide on a furniture joint: you can see that it is important to learn how to use each kind of plane, and not take off too much wood.

Planes can either be referred to by name or by a series of numbers. See pages 56 and 57 for further information on how to sharpen the blade.

Note the try plane, jack plane and fore plane are all sharpened and honed so that the plane blade is convex (see page 57).

JACK PLANE

There are two basic sizes – the No.5 (2in (50mm) wide blade) and the No.5½ (2⅜in (60mm) wide blade). The primary functions of a jack plane are to remove excess wood, and to smooth and flatten rough-sawn or distorted wood (page 66). Before you use a jack plane, the wood should be dry and secondary conditioned (see page 12). A jack plane is a medium-length plane – 14–15in (355–380mm) – meaning that it is light enough to work with for long periods of time, yet still long enough to level out bumps. See page 67 for the correct method of using a jack plane.

TRY PLANE OR JOINTER PLANE

The basic size is the No.7 (2⅜in (60mm) wide blade). A try plane is longer than a jack plane – 22in (560mm) – and is used to make long edges straight; to correct edges that are out of square; and for the edge jointing of boards (see page 75). If sharpened and set up properly, the edge that the try plane produces can be adjusted and made true, independent of any adjacent faces (see page 68). If you are careful, you can work to very fine tolerances, and take off just one shaving at a time to produce a perfect edge joint.

THE PARTS OF A BENCH PLANE

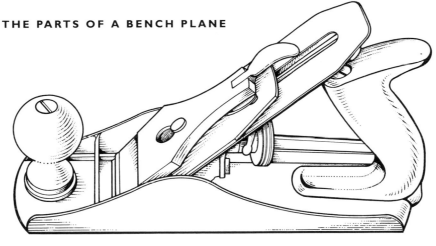

frog
assembly

frog
adjustment
screw

FORE PLANE

The basic size is the No.6 (2⅜in (60mm) wide blade). The fore plane is longer than the jack plane but shorter than the try plane — 18in (460mm) — and thus is an ideal in–between plane, able to perform the jobs of both the other planes. The fore plane can be sharpened and set in different ways, according to the type of work.

SMOOTHING PLANE

The sizes are the No.3 (1¾in (45mm) wide blade), No.4 (2in (50mm) wide blade), and No.4½ (2⅜in (60mm) wide blade). A smoothing plane is used for cleaning up and to flatten out any ridges left by the jack, fore or try planes. The end of the blade is sharpened so that it is straight rather than convex, with its two corners dubbed off to stop the edges of the blade digging into the wood. The set on a good smoothing plane can be altered from coarse to extremely fine by using the frog adjustment (see right). When working, plane the surface following the direction of grain rather than from one end of a piece of wood to the other. This could mean working at an angle across the surface of the wood, or using a slicing, circular motion (for the technique see page 88).

By releasing the frog locking screws (underneath the plane blade) and adjusting the frog assembly, the mouth of the plane can be altered, increasing or decreasing the amount of cut

HOW TO SET A PLANE

Shaded areas show width of mouth

coarser cut: mouth more open

finer cut: mouth more closed

plane blade

cap iron

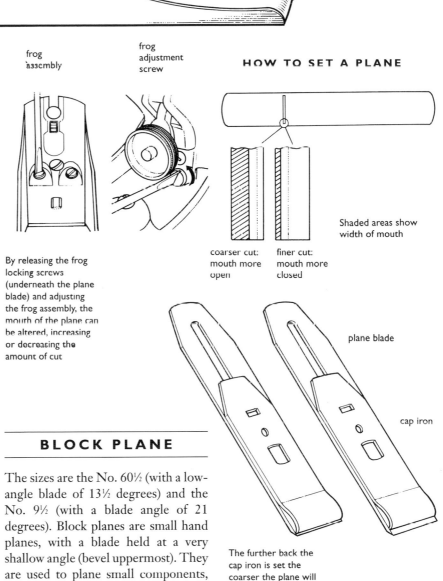

The further back the cap iron is set the coarser the plane will cut

BLOCK PLANE

The sizes are the No. 60½ (with a low-angle blade of 13½ degrees) and the No. 9½ (with a blade angle of 21 degrees). Block planes are small hand planes, with a blade held at a very shallow angle (bevel uppermost). They are used to plane small components, including composite sheet materials, and specifically the end grain of solid wood. Block planes have only a single iron (plane blade), rather than a double iron (plane blade and cap iron) as in the case of most bench planes.

SPECIAL PLANES

As with most tools, some planes have been developed to perform special tasks. Here are just a few...

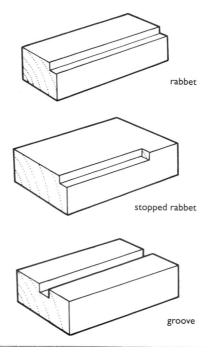

rabbet

stopped rabbet

groove

RABBET PLANE

A bench rabbet plane has a mouth which extends across the entire width of the sole of the plane. This enables a rabbet (sometimes called a rebate) to be worked, usually along the grain from one end of a piece of wood to the other. Rabbet planes vary in length from 9¼in (235mm) to 13in (330mm). Some rabbet planes actually have a knife (cutting spur) to score the fibers of the wood, ready for working across the grain as well as along it. To help keep the rabbet size accurate, some rabbet planes have adjustable depth and fence gauges. These are known as fillister planes.

SHOULDER PLANE

Shoulder planes are smaller than rabbet planes and have a shallow cutting angle for working across the grain. They do not usually have depth and fence gauges as they are used for the cleaning up of shoulders of joints, especially when fitting wide tenons and dado joints. Some shoulder planes have removable fronts to convert them into a 'chisel plane', which can be used to work into the corner of a stopped rabbet. A variation on the shoulder plane is the bullnose plane, which is shorter and has a much smaller sole in front of the actual cutting edge.

1 Bench plane blade
2 Honing guide
3 Bench rabbet plane
4 Combination/ plough plane
5 Cabinet makers shoulder plane
6 Spokeshave
7 Scraper plane
8 Cabinet makers bullnose plane
9 Router plane

HOW TO ADJUST A WOODEN PLANE

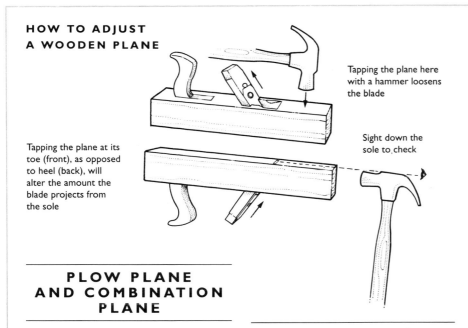

Tapping the plane at its toe (front), as opposed to heel (back), will alter the amount the blade projects from the sole

Tapping the plane here with a hammer loosens the blade

Sight down the sole to check

PLOW PLANE AND COMBINATION PLANE

A plow plane cuts grooves, whereas a combination plane combines the jobs of both rabbet and plow planes. It may also have extra profile cutters for producing beadings or for tongue and groove work.

SCRAPER PLANE

This is sometimes called a cabinet scraper although, being strictly accurate, a true scraper is a piece of tool steel with burred-over edges. The scraper plane performs the same function as the traditional hand cabinet scraper – i.e. it removes torn grain – but its rigid body does not give the same flexibility and control. However, scraper planes are generally easier to work with, and on surfaces that are to be heavily scraped there is no risk of fatigue (hand cabinet scrapers may well make your thumbs sore and can even cause blisters). See page 35.

ROUTER PLANE

Router planes have a blade set below the sole, allowing it to fit comfortably into a groove or dado. They are especially handy for cleaning out the long trenches which run across the grain in traditional through and stopped dado joints.

SPOKESHAVE

There are two main sorts of spokeshave. The first is a flat-based (or straight-faced) spokeshave, which is used to smooth convex edges. The second is the round-based (or round-faced) spokeshave, which will clean up and prepare concave edges. There is a special skill to using spokeshaves, which takes time to practice: this is the reason why in inexperienced hands they have a tendency to chatter along the surface of the wood (usually caused by the blade protruding too far from the sole). It is common to push a spokeshave away from you during use although many craftsmen prefer to use it on the pull stroke.

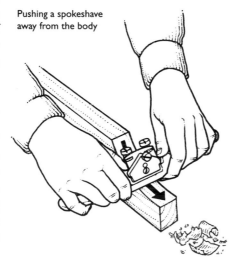

Pushing a spokeshave away from the body

For the technique of honing, see page 57.

HONING GUIDE

Mastering the skills of sharpening plane blades and chisels can take time and lots of practice. The skills are not difficult to learn but it can be frustrating when the final cutting edge is not how you intended it to be. Honing guides hold the blade being sharpened at a steady angle, which takes away the guesswork and allows you to concentrate on pushing the blade backward and forward. The only disadvantage to using a guide is that because the wheel actually runs on the stone, in effect this reduces the length of it. You must therefore be careful not to let the stone become hollow or uneven during sharpening. For the technique of honing, see page 57.

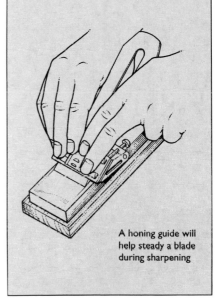

A honing guide will help steady a blade during sharpening

TIP

Although the blade of a bench plane may give years of good service, at some point in time you may need to order a new one. The following information should help you.

The standard length of a bench plane blade is usually 7¼in (185mm), but the width varies depending on the type of plane. These are usually 1¾in (45mm), 2in (50mm), 2⅛in (55mm) or 2⅜in (60mm) and when ordering blades, this size must be specified. It is also wise to tell the supplier the model/product number of the plane.

THE CABINET SCRAPER

When hand planing, even with a sharp, finely set blade, it is still possible to pull out the fibers of the wood. This produces torn grain, which is a direct result of the fibers running through a board in many different directions. Fortunately, this defect can easily be rectified with a cabinet scraper. It is important to learn the proper techniques of preparing, using, and sharpening a scraper or you could very well create more problems than those produced by the bench planes in the first place.

PREPARING A SCRAPER FOR USE

1 First of all, put the scraper in a vise with one of the long flat edges uppermost. Take a medium/fine file and use it to file from one end of the scraper to the other. This will keep the edge square and flat.

2 Next, draw-file lightly along the edge of the scraper to remove any coarse file marks. Turn the cabinet scraper over and prepare the second long edge as above.

3 On the top of a fine oil stone remove the four burrs that have been produced (one long edge has two sides). Keep the side of the scraper flat against the stone and use firm pressure, pushing backward and forward.

4 Put the lid on the oil stone box and, using this as a jig, push the scraper against the side of the stone to prepare two polished, square edges. Clean any excess oil from the scraper.

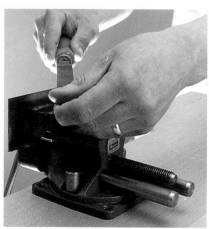

1

2

3

4

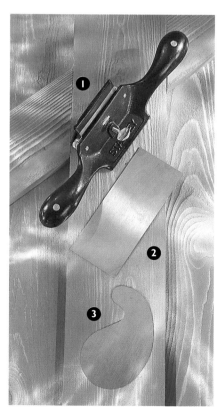

1 Scraper plane
2 Cabinet scraper
3 Goose-neck cabinet scraper

HOW TO USE A BURNISHER TO SHARPEN A SCRAPER

A burnisher is also known as a ticketer.
The technique of sharpening a scraper requires practice.

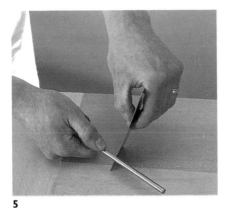

5

6

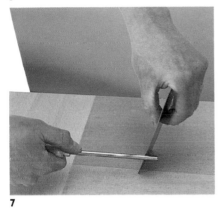

7

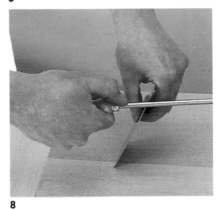

8

5 and 6 Hold the cabinet scraper, resting one of the short edges in the palm of your left hand, and have the other short edge pushing against a bench top. Flex the scraper slightly with your thumb. Hold the burnisher at around 70 degrees to the front face of the scraper and draw it firmly toward you along the side to be sharpened, starting from near the bottom. Push the burnisher against the scraper as if sharpening a knife with a steel. But never use a knife steel or screwdriver shank to sharpen a scraper.

7 and 8 Repeat this process for the back of the scraper but this time push away from you at an angle of 70 degrees, again from near the bottom.

Next, turn the scraper right over so that the other short end rests on the bench, and burr over the front and then the back, as before. This will result in two strokes in total being delivered at the center. Repeat this to sharpen both sides of the other long edge of the scraper. This produces four cutting edges in total.

IMPORTANT Do not turn the edge of the scraper over too much with the burnisher – one or two strokes per side is usually enough. You may fail with sharpening a scraper because you have rounded the edge over too much. If you have burred over the edge too much, go right back to stage 1 and re-file.

If you do not push hard enough and so have not turned the edge sufficiently you can repeat the process from the burnisher stage only. A little light machine oil or spit may help to lubricate the burnisher.

TIP
When scraping a small area of torn grain, work a larger area to create, in effect, an extremely shallow dip. This easily sands out.

HOW TO USE A SCRAPER

When you use a jack plane, the convex plane blade creates small ridges running along the surface of the wood. The smoothing plane removes these marks, but may tear up the grain slightly as it does so. A cabinet scraper will remove this defect.

Never scrape along the length of the wood. This will create more small ridges on the wood, which are very difficult to sand out. Scrape the wood at constantly varying angles to the edges of the wood, but never scrape directly across or along the grain.

Hold the scraper with both hands in a relaxed manner, using your thumbs to flex it (see photograph below). The more you bend the scraper, the more it cuts.

Hold it at an angle between 30 degrees and 45 degrees to the surface of the wood, although the exact angle will depend on the burr produced during sharpening. The lower the angle at which you hold the scraper, the more it cuts. Beware of holding it too low, because it will dig in. The angle and the degree to which you flex the scraper, determine together the total amount of cut as you work.

After scraping the surface, it is preferable to sand the wood along the grain by hand, using 80/100 grit garnet paper. Work through the grades carefully using finer and finer papers as you progress (see page 90).

THE STANLEY SURFORM

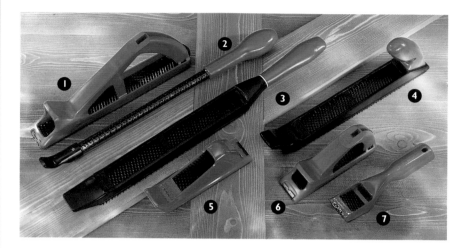

1 Surform molded body plane 2 Surform round file 3 Surform flat file 4 Surform metal body plane 5 Surform metal body block plane 6 Surform molded body block plane 7 Surform molded body shaver tool

The Surform is a specially designed tool for rasping, trimming and filing curved and compound shapes. Surforms do not take the place of good quality bench planes; instead they have about 450 teeth on a standard-cut 10in (255mm) blade, which cut away at the wood like miniature chisels. Surforms do not need sharpening or adjusting during use. The Stanley Surform is a safe and versatile tool and does not require any special skill to use. It is especially suitable for shaping and smoothing unusual patterns and moldings.

The Surform is available both as a metal-bodied tool, or in strong plastic (glass reinforced polypropylene). There are many different varieties of Surform, suitable for a wide range of jobs.

SURFORM SPECIFICATIONS

Metal body	Surforms o/a length in	Length of blade in
Planer file	12.2	9.85
Plane	12.4	9.85
Flat file	17.3	9.85
Block plane	6.1	5.5
Round file	14.3	9.85

Molded body thumb screw for blade release		
Flat file	11.8	5.5
Plane	10.6	9.85
Block plane	6.1	5.5
Shaver tool	7.3	2.5

standard

half round

fine

metal/plastic

Surform blade types for different degrees of finish

round

curved

HAMMERS AND MALLETS

There is more to hammers and mallets than the apparent simplicity of pounding in a nail might lead us to believe.

HAMMERS

A well made and properly used hammer will last for many years. A hammer should have a comfortable, well balanced, shock-resistant handle, and the striking face of the head should be hardened – after all, it stands to reason that a hammer should be harder than the object it's hitting.

When using a hammer, always deliver a fair blow. The face of the hammer should hit the object, whether a nail or a wooden block, square on. Select the correct hammer type and weight for the job (see page 38) and make sure you do not accidentally damage or hit the handle when you are performing heavier duty tasks.

MALLETS

The mallets used in woodworking are usually made of wood themselves, and unlike hammers, they never have a steel head. The reason for this is simple – mallets are specifically designed to be used with tools, offering them protection but still allowing complete control. In order to increase their weight, carpenter's mallets (used to chop out joints) have a large head and are often made from beech, a wood which is close grained, quite hard and very resistant to impact.

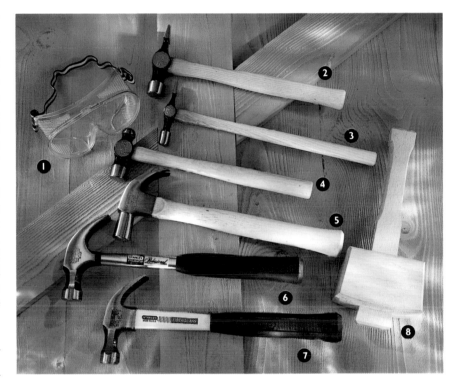

1 Safety goggles
2 Cross-peen Warrington Pattern hammer
3 Pin or telephone hammer
4 Ball-peen hammer
5 Wooden handled claw hammer
6 Steel handled claw hammer
7 Fiberglass handled claw hammer
8 Carpenter's mallet

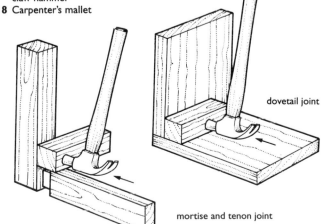

dovetail joint

Use a hammer and block to separate joints – always deliver a fair blow to the center of the block

mortise and tenon joint

HAMMER TYPES

Through the generations, dozens of hammer types have been developed. Some are very specialized and the layman could have fun guessing what they could be used for; others are far more familiar.

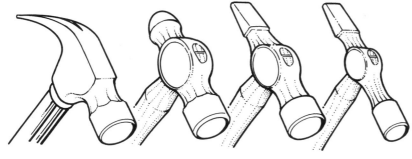

claw hammer

ball-peen
(engineer's)
hammer

cross-peen
(Warrington)
hammer

tack hammer

CLAW

weight	13oz (365g); 16oz (450g); 20oz (570g); 24oz (680g)
use	general purpose carpentry; insertion and removal of nails
look for	head – forged, polished, heat-treated steel; handle – tubular steel or wooden, well-secured to head

TACK

weight	3½oz (100g); 4oz (115g)
use	light duty work including driving in of tacks and veneer pins
look for	head – see claw hammers; handle – see cross-peen hammers

BALL-PEEN

weight	various from 4oz (110g) – 48oz (1360g)
use	metal working
look for	head and handle – see claw hammers

CROSS-PEEN (WARRINGTON)

weight	6oz (170g); 8oz (230g); 10oz (280g); 12oz (340g); 14oz (400g); 16oz (450g)
use	cabinet work and finish carpentry; driving some nails and brads into awkward areas
look for	head – see claw hammers; handle – wooden (ash or hickory) for shock absorption

HOW TO USE A CARPENTER'S MALLET

For chopping out mortises, use a controlled clean stroke. Do not lift the mallet much more than 12in (300mm) from the chisel handle between blows – if you strike from any higher than this, you will lose control. Use the face of the mallet for most work, although you can use the the side of the mallet head (or the palm of your hand) to tap the chisel gently during the cleaning up of joints.

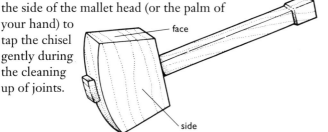

face

side

GOOD HABITS

Do not use a mallet to knock joints apart, as its square corners will damage the work and the flat face will spread the blow – use a hammer.

For the greatest control, always strike a chisel with the center of the mallet face, never near its edges.

HOW HAMMERS ARE MADE

A well-made hammer should be well finished, comfortable and have perfect balance - it is only the care taken at the manufacturing stage that guarantees this every time.

All Stanley hammer heads are electronically smelted and then drop-forged in a 600 ton press, ensuring that the grain pattern of the steel follows the shape of the head. This reduces the risk of damage and chipping. Good quality hammers are heat-treated by quenching: in the case of claw hammers, the claws are quenched in oil, whereas the polls are quenched in water. This guarantees the right degree of hardness and greatly reduces metal fatigue.

Once the hammer head has been made, ground and polished, the next stage is to fit the handle. Wooden handles are made from hickory or ash, the grains of which are selected for strength. First, the moisture level at the end of the handle is reduced; then it is sealed with oil. Once it has been inserted under pressure into the eye of the hammer head, the handle is secured by a combination of hard wood and steel wedges, which are driven into place under a weight of 8 tons. If tubular steel handles are fitted, these are driven into place by a 5 ton press and swaged for a truly permanent fixing.

Hammer heads being manufactured at the Stanley factory

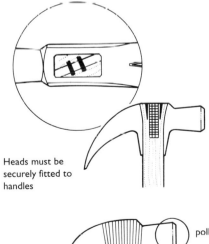

Heads must be securely fitted to handles

Heat treatment of heads guarantees the correct degree of hardness on both the face and claw

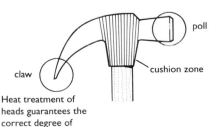

claw

poll

cushion zone

Forged heads (see below) ensure the grain structure of the steel flows with the shape of the hammer head for extra strength. Heads that have not been forged are very susceptible to damage

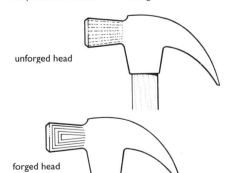

unforged head

forged head

SHOPPING GUIDE

ESSENTIAL TOOLS

16OZ (450G) CLAW HAMMER For general purpose work.

8 OR 10OZ (230 OR 280G) WARRINGTON HAMMER For use with small nails and pins. Warrington hammers are ideal for knocking joints apart but remember to protect the workpiece with a block.

SUGGESTED ADDITIONAL TOOLS

TACK HAMMER To drive home very small brads in fine or light duty work.

CHISELS

There are three basic types of chisel. These are firmer chisels,
bevel-edged paring chisels, and mortise chisels. Each was originally designed to
perform distinctly different tasks.

TRADITIONAL CHISELS

FIRMER CHISELS

Traditionally made with square edges to the blade, which provided extra strength for work such as chopping out joints. As this usually meant being hit with a mallet, they are of strong construction. The handle, usually wooden, has a ferrule where the blade tang enters the handle and may be strengthened at the top to prevent splitting.

BEVEL-EDGED CHISELS

More slender than firmer chisels, having the edges of the blade chamfered off, allowing the chisel to be worked into corners, and thus especially useful for cleaning up joints. These chisels were originally not intended to be hit with a mallet, and the wooden handle was not usually strengthened. A paring chisel is a specific type of bevel-edged chisel, being longer and more slender still, giving the craftsman extra control to work back to a line, accurately pushing with the weight of the upper body. With a well sharpened chisel, body weight would usually be enough to cut through the wood cleanly.

1 Bevel edge paring chisel
2 Wooden handled firmer chisel
3 Polypropylene handle firmer chisel
Bevel edged chisels
4 ¼in/6mm carver handle
5 ½in/12mm carver handle
6 1in/25mm carver handle
7 ¼in/6mm molded handle
8 ½in/12mm molded handle
9 ¾in/18mm molded handle
10 1in/25mm molded handle

MORTISE CHISELS

Much stronger than other types, having a thicker blade that is long and tapered so that it can be levered to remove waste during the chopping of deep mortises.

All three basic types of chisel are still available today, some made to original patterns, depending on the manufacturer. But with the development of new materials there have been changes too. Handles are now often made from polypropylene, a plastic of immense strength. Some woodworkers still prefer the feel of wooden handles, but plastic handles are certainly much stronger and more resistant to impact.

Modern steel bevel-edged chisels can often perform the tasks of both the traditional firmer and bevel-edged chisels. Chisels such as the Stanley 5002 series, for example, can safely be used for heavy duty jobs as well as much more delicate work. However, if you are ever in any doubt about a particular range, always refer to individual manufacturer's instructions.

HANDLE TYPES

There are three main types of chisel handle. Always try out the feel of the handle before you buy: a good chisel should feel comfortable and well-balanced.

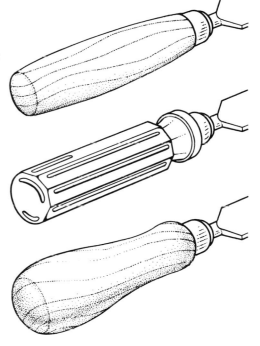

CARVER The traditional style of handle for bevel-edged and paring chisels. Available in either wood or plastic.

OCTAGONAL Usually wooden but not quite as comfortable to use as the carver handle. Designed to stop the chisel rolling off the workbench.

OVAL The oval section stops the chisel rolling around on the workbench. A heavier duty pattern than the carver handle.

BEWARE

Don't be fooled by looks. A chisel, particularly with a traditional wooden handle, may give the impression of good quality, but this does not mean that it is necessarily well made. It is a good policy to purchase only well known, top brand names. On poorer quality chisels, the blade may not be hardened correctly (or at all) and in extreme cases it will bend or break during use. If you are unable to sharpen a chisel properly because it is poorly made, you will never achieve a good, keen cut and the result is a tool that is more or less useless for the purpose for which you bought it.

WHAT MAKES A GOOD CHISEL

FEATURE	WHAT TO LOOK FOR
Top quality steel blade hardened and tempered, flat ground faces	Chisel blades should be capable of achieving a keen edge during sharpening. The strength and reliability of the steel are critical. Stanley chisels are made from chrome alloy, a steel similar to that used in the manufacture of ball bearings
Balance	A chisel should feel well balanced and comfortable, becoming in effect an extension of your hand
Handle	The handle should feel comfortable and be capable of withstanding blows with a mallet
Secure handle fixing	It is important that the handle cannot twist or work loose during use. On the Stanley 5002 series the bolster and tang are friction-welded together. Even under destructive testing where the blade is bent to 45 degrees, the weld should still not fail

HOW TO USE A CHISEL

Chisels are designed to cut or chop away at wood and to do this
they are either struck with a mallet or pushed into the wood. For example,
when cutting deep mortises, a mallet will provide extra force, whereas
when cleaning up or working back to a line (paring), the weight of your
body will usually be enough.

VERTICAL PARING

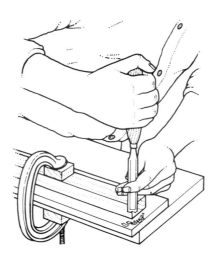

Vertical paring means working from above and pushing the chisel down, on to and through the wood, to remove a corner or small edge, or to work back to a marking line.

1 First fasten the workpiece to a bench with a C-clamp (make sure you put a scrap of wood on top of and underneath the workpiece as protection) – see page 53.

2 Sandwich the chisel blade (about 1½in (38mm) from the end) in your left hand between your thumb and your index finger, with your thumb at the back.

3 Put your middle finger just below your index finger at the back of the chisel, below your thumb. The chisel should rest against the middle third of your middle finger.

> ### IMPORTANT
>
> The left hand controls the chisel, the right provides the push and strength.
>
> Do not try to take off more than ½₂in to ¹⁄₁₆in at a time.

4 Use these two fingers and your thumb to hold the chisel firmly, for proper control. You can use your ring finger in addition to your middle finger for extra power.

5 Rest your left hand on top of the workpiece with the chisel edge above the part to be pared off. Position your little finger slightly behind the others for comfort. Do not attempt to take off too much wood at once and carefully work back to a knife line.

6 Next, lean over the chisel with your body so that your right shoulder is over the chisel handle. Hold the chisel handle firmly in your right hand.

7 Either use just your right hand to push down on the chisel, or for extra force gently use the weight of your shoulder, pushing against your right hand to pare off the waste.

HORIZONTAL PARING

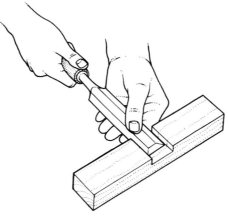

Horizontal paring is performed when you are cleaning out the bottom of joints, such as the half-lap joint. It is always best to hold the workpiece steady in a vise (see page 54).

1 Put the joint to be cleaned up into the vise just above the marking gauge line to which you are working.

2 Let the chisel blade rest (bevel edge up) across all four fingers of your left hand (palm uppermost), lying roughly against the bottom third of your

fingers. Your left hand gives the control. Hold the chisel in place with your thumb about half-way down.

3 Either push the chisel into the wood using the pad of your right hand against the handle (perhaps lightly tapping the chisel with this fleshy part of your hand), or firmly grip the handle with your right hand and push toward the wood. The aim is gently to push or strike the chisel handle, carefully cutting into the wood.

Do not work all the way across the joint from one edge to the other or the fibers will tear out on the back edge. Instead, work just past halfway through and turn the piece of wood around so that you cut from both edges. Make sure that the bottom of the joint is flat by gently cleaning up with a chisel

HOW TO USE A MALLET AND MORTISE CHISEL TO CHOP A MORTISE

Always clamp the work firmly (see page 53). It is important that the workpiece is not allowed to slip while you are using a mallet and chisel. Always mortise to the exact width of the mortise chisel itself and adjust the dimensions of the joint to match the chisels you have.

Hold the chisel upright in your left hand with the bevel edge facing away from you. Wrap all your fingers around the chisel handle with your knuckles facing away from you. Hold the chisel firmly but relax your grip slightly for comfort.

Standing behind or just to one side of the workpiece, hold the mallet in your right hand and deliver a firm blow to the chisel handle. Do not use a hammer. Always keep the chisel perfectly upright and at 90 degrees to

the surface of the wood (test with a square if necessary). After the first blow move the chisel back slightly and strike the chisel again. Any waste from the second blow will be left in the hole produced by the first strike. Remove this as you go by pulling back on the chisel.

Start from the center of the mortise, working in one direction toward you. After a few strikes turn the chisel around completely so that the bevel is facing you and remove the other half of the mortise by working away from you.

Make sure you leave a small amount of waste at both ends of the mortise for cleaning up by paring vertically. See page 37 for more details on hammers and mallets, and page 77 for more on removing waste.

See page 37 for more details on hammers and mallets, and page 77 for more on removing waste.

TECHNICAL TALK

FRICTION-WELDING If sufficient heat is generated by friction two components can be joined. In the case of Stanley chisels the joint between the blade and the bolster is friction-welded by spinning them together at 2500 rpm, instantly locking them together.

SHOPPING GUIDE

ESSENTIAL TOOLS

5002 SERIES CHISELS: ¼in (6mm); ½in (12mm); ¾in (18mm); 1in (25mm). Essential for cutting and cleaning up joints in basic woodworking.

SUGGESTED ADDITIONAL TOOLS

5002 SERIES CHISELS: ⅛in (4mm); ⅜in (10mm); ⅝in (16mm). The first is not available in the Stanley 5002 range.

MORTISE CHISEL: ¼in (6mm).

HAND DRILLS AND BRACES

There are two basic hand tools which, in conjunction with a variety of drill bits, bore holes in wood. These are known as either a hand drill (the breast drill being essentially a large hand drill) or a brace.

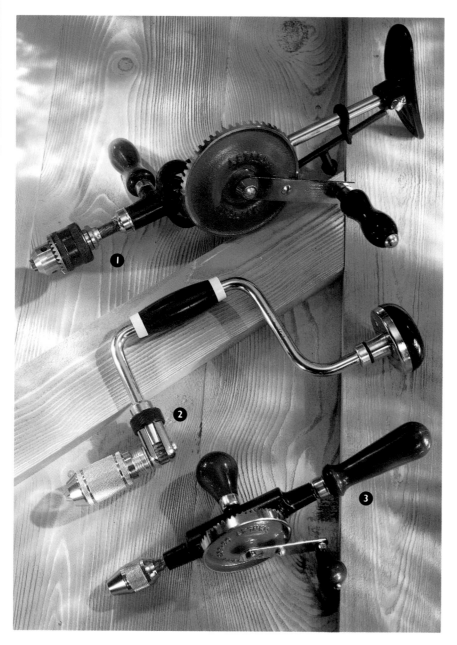

1 Breast drill
2 Ratchet brace
3 Hand drill

The brace is a larger and more heavy-duty tool than the hand drill. The brace is intended for use with large drill bits – augers, for example – and is able to drill deep holes. The much faster rotating hand drill is used with smaller twist drill bits.

At the business end of each tool is a chuck which tightens on to the drill bit, holding it firm and allowing it to bite into the wood without slipping. Note that each chuck is designed to accept only a certain type of bit (see page 46). The chuck can develop quite a grip on the bit during use; if you follow the procedure described opposite you will be able to remove the bit more easily after use.

WHEN TO USE A HAND DRILL

The hand drill has gearing to increase its chuck speed and permit fast boring of small holes. It is only suitable for straight shank drill bits (twist drills) and for some 'special' drill bits, including countersink bits. Hand drills are most often used to drill pilot and clearance holes for wood screws.

WHEN TO USE A BRACE

A brace works slowly, one revolution of the handle being one turn of the chuck. The cranked handle offers a lot of leverage and the brace is built to drill deep, wide holes, slowly and accurately. Some braces have ratchet attachments that will allow you to work up against a cabinet side or wall. Expansive bits, which will allow you to bore very wide holes, can be used safely in a brace.

THE SIMPLEST BORERS OF WOOD

BRADAWL

A very simple tool, essentially a length of round wire flattened at one end and fastened into a handle. It is used to make starter holes for drilling and inserting screws. Place the flattened end across the fibers of the wood to break them and twist the tool while pushing to open up the hole.

GIMLET

A particularly useful tool, having a drill bit with a screw tip. The screw helps to pull the gimlet into the wood whilst the drill clears out waste from the hole. It is able to produce deeper and more accurate starter holes than a bradawl.

---

1 Adjustable expansive bit
2 Centre bit – taper shank
3 Auger bit – taper shank
4 Twist drill set
5 Screwsink combination counterbore
6 Screwmate drill and countersink
7 Rosehead countersink
8 Plug cutter

HOW TO INSERT AND REMOVE DRILL BITS

HAND DRILL

To remove drill bits, hold the hand drill chuck firmly in your left hand. Grip the drive handle in your right. Turn it toward you in a counterclockwise direction. By suddenly stopping the chuck turning, you will release the drill bit. You may find it helpful to steady the hand drill against your body which will give extra pulling power. To insert a drill bit, do the same operation in reverse.

BRACE

The method is essentially the same as for the hand drill above. Hold the chuck in your left hand and, steadying the brace against your body, turn the cranked handle counterclockwise, by pulling toward you. Use firm pressure. If you do this in reverse it will tighten the chuck.

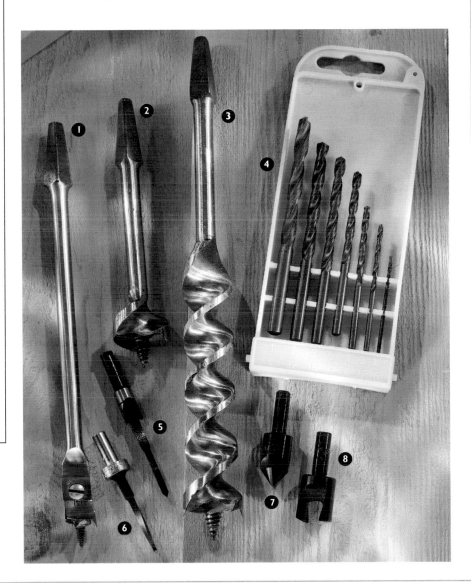

HOW TO USE A HAND DRILL

Always stay in control by clamping the workpiece to the bench or holding it steady in a vise.

A sharp drill bit will easily cut through wood without any excessive pushing, although if the bit is not kept at 90 degrees to the surface, it will bind in the hole and stop turning. When drilling small holes, hold the hand drill with the drive handle in your right hand and use your left hand to hold the steadying handle (the one at the opposite end of the drill from the chuck). You may need to use a little extra pressure from your body but do not overdo this. Use a square or some other guide, if necessary, to ensure that you are working at the correct angle to the surface.

Before starting to drill, mark the exact

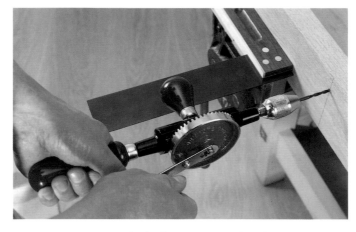

position of the hole on the wood with a sharp steel awl. This will stop the bit from wandering across the surface of the wood as you start turning the drive handle. If you prefer to make the pin-

point a little larger, turn the drive handle carefully backward for a quarter to half of a turn, before starting to drill forward in the normal way. Always turn the drill slowly to begin with, only

gathering speed as the bit begins to bite.

The third handle provides extra pushing power when drilling deeper holes, though do not push too hard, as this will reduce the amount of control you have.

If you are drilling all the way through a piece of wood, it is important not to let the back of the work splinter out. To stop this, clamp a backup board firmly behind the wood.

To help remove the drill bit from the wood after drilling, move your left hand (after drilling) to the third handle (opposite the drive handle). This will stop the hand drill spinning and allow you to pull the drill from the wood. Continue turning the drive handle clockwise while backing out from the drill hole.

HOW TO USE A BRACE

The brace is most often used with an auger bit, which has a screw end to position it exactly and to help pull the bit into the wood. The nickers or spurs around the end of the bit actually score the wood as it turns, and the waste in-between the screw and these spurs is scooped out by the cutting edges. A sharp auger will slowly cut a deep, wide, accurate hole in both softwoods and hardwoods. Mark the starting position with an awl or center punch and start to drill by allowing the screw thread to bite into the wood at this point.

Hold the wood to be drilled in a vise, as near to the jaws as possible, as this will provide extra rigidity. Use firm body pressure to help push the drill bit through the wood as you turn the cranked handle clockwise.

Before going all the way through the workpiece, keep checking to see when

the screw thread on the drill bit just becomes visible on the other side. At this point, remove the drill by turning it counterclockwise. Turn the workpiece around in the vise. Drill into the same hole again, this time through the exit hole left by the auger screw. Never push so hard against the brace that you lose control. Let the drill bit do the work.

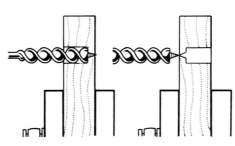

When using a brace and auger bit, drill into the front face until the screw is just visible at the back . . .

. . . then turn the wood around and drill from the back into the exit hole left by the auger screw

JAWS IN BRACES

The design of the jaws of a chuck guarantees that they grip a drill bit to stop it turning. Jaws will hold only certain types of drill bit and here is a guide to which ones do what.

UNIVERSAL JAWS

Some jaw types, known as universal jaws, are able to hold No 1 morse taper bits, straight shank (twist drills) as well as the more usual auger bits. In case of doubt, refer to the manufacturer's instructions.

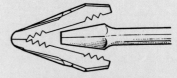

ALLIGATOR JAWS

The jaws of most braces are designed to hold only square taper shank auger bits and will not accept or grip on to other kinds of drill bit.

DON'T DRILL TOO DEEP

If you accidentally drill a screw hole too deep, before putting in the screw, mix a stiff paste of fine wood dust and glue and squeeze it well into the hole before inserting the wood screw. As the glue dries, the screw will be held securely.

Drilling too far altogether, and allowing the drill bit to pop through the other side of the workpiece is a bigger problem – not very pretty on a table top! Any gadget to help prevent this has got to be good: the illustrations here give some ideas.

The simplest method is to mark the drill bit indicating where you need to stop; either wrap masking tape around it or paint on paper white-out fluid at the appropriate point. The disadvantage is that as the tape or paper white-out fluid wears off, if you are not careful, you can actually find yourself drilling deeper and deeper as you progress from one hole to another.

Alternatively, if you have a twist drill, you can use a drill stop. This looks a little like a large washer, which you fasten on the drill bit by means of a small screw. Beware, however – if the drill stop touches the workpiece while spinning, it will damage it. Overcome this by using a thin piece of plywood or card, with a hole drilled in it, to protect the wood surface.

A drill block, a square piece of wood with a protruding arm (used as a handle) on one side to stop it spinning around, will both protect the wood and determine how far you drill

1 *Left* Wrap tape or mark the drill bit with paper correction fluid at the correct depth

2 *Right* A drill stop will determine how far to drill but take care not to damage the surface of the wood

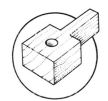

3 A drill block is safe to use and will determine how deep you drill according to its thickness

by its thickness. There is absolutely no risk of damage but making the block can be fiddly and time-consuming.

TECHNICAL TALK

TWIST DRILLS A simple parallel/cylindrical drill bit for drilling pilot and clearance holes for screws. Used in hand drills, electric drills and some braces.

AUGERS A type of bit which cuts much larger and wider holes than twist drills. Must be used only in braces as these revolve very slowly.

EXPANSIVE BIT An adjustable type of auger bit for drilling a wide range of hole widths.

CENTER BIT Looks very similar to an auger but does not have the helical twist which would allow it to drill deep holes. Only suitable for shallow, clean-looking holes.

PLUG CUTTER Used in either a power drill or an electrical drill press. Creates decorative plugs that fit into counter-bored holes concealing screw heads.

COUNTERSINK BIT Cuts tapered recessed holes that permit a countersunk screw head to lie flush or slightly below the surface of the wood. The clearance hole must be drilled first to guide the bit before countersinking.

CLEARANCE HOLE A wider hole than a pilot hole, allowing the main body of the screw to fit comfortably through it.

PILOT HOLE Small hole used to guide the screw, allowing it to bite without splitting the wood.

PLUGGING

This is a technique for occasions when a screw-head or hole is to be hidden by a wooden plug.

A plug cutter produces a small cylindrical piece of wood with the grain running across its face. This is different from a dowel, where the grain runs along its length and provides strength. Plugs are easy to make. Use a plug cutter to drill into a scrap piece of wood. It will automatically stop at a certain depth. Next, simply break off the plug with a screwdriver.

To bore the hole into which the plug will fit (counterboring):

• Use a twist drill bit of the same diameter as the plug to bore a wider hole into the clearance hole, see page 51.

• Or, better still, use an auger bit of the same diameter as the plug, letting the point of the auger mark the exact position where you will drill the pilot and clearance holes later.

Insert the screw into its counterbored hole, tap the plug into place and clean off with a hand plane. You can use a little glue to hold the plug in position. Ensure that its figure and color match the surrounding wood.

SHOPPING GUIDE

ESSENTIAL TOOLS

HAND DRILL Buy only a well-engineered smooth-running hand drill with twin pinions to support the driving wheel, preferably with an enclosed body. Should accept twist drills up to 5⁄16in (8mm) diameter.

ADDITIONAL TOOLS

BRACE Must be well engineered, preferably with a ratchet attachment for ease of use. Should accept taper shank auger bits up to 7⁄8in (22mm) diameter.

SCREWDRIVERS

There is a very easy way of completely ruining a perfect piece of work. Simply select a screwdriver with a damaged tip or choose one of the wrong size, and then use it to drive in a screw.

Screwdrivers are probably the most misused hand tool in every day use. The problem is that being handy, they can be used for just about every job that a chisel could be used for (but to less effect) and they are perfect, are they not, as steel wedges for pulling two chunks of wood apart and for opening cans of paint.

I was once fitting some doors on a cabinet in our workshop, when a plumber working on the building asked me whether I had a large screwdriver he could borrow. If I had not asked him how large he actually meant I would not have discovered he simply wanted it to knock a brick off a wall … I figure my tools had rather a close call there.

The real truth of the matter is that if you use a screwdriver for anything other than driving in screws you will almost inevitably cause irreparable damage to it.

If you want to produce quality woodwork, make sure that you always look after your screwdrivers properly and they will go on working perfectly for years.

TRADITIONAL SCREWDRIVERS

Logically, the story of the screwdriver starts with that of the screw. Early wood screws were made by hand and were relatively crude affairs, easily identified by their flattened tips. Screws were no longer made by hand after around 1850, when mass-produced screws with fine machined pointed tips began to appear. As engineering standards improved generally, so did the tools used to drive screws into wood.

The essence of the screwdriver is this. A round or square bar is flattened at one end into a blade that fits a slot in the screw. Simple. The bar is hardened and tempered for strength. Top quality screwdrivers have forged tips, precision ground to fit manufactured screws exactly. Then they may be polished, to improve their appearance.

There are two major types of screwdriver tip, the first being the slotted type just described, and the second a more modern invention, the Phillips or crosspoint. This tip is specially designed to prevent the screwdriver slipping and damaging the work. A third type, the square drive or Robertson, is common in Canada and is becoming popular in the U.S. as well.

HANDLES

Screwdriver handles are often made from injection-moulded polypropylene, rather than wood. This guarantees that the handle is virtually unbreakable and allows the shank to fit securely into the handle. Plastic has not yet entirely superseded wood, however; wooden-handled cabinet screwdrivers are still made in vast quantities and many professional woodworkers prefer the feel of wood. Wooden-handled screwdrivers are generally made from round bar (see opposite), the handle being fastened in place using a traditional bolster construction process.

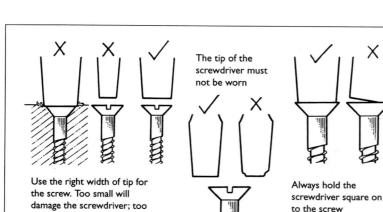

Use the right width of tip for the screw. Too small will damage the screwdriver; too large will damage the wood

The tip of the screwdriver must not be worn

Always hold the screwdriver square on to the screw

DO'S AND DON'TS

DO stop driving in a screw if it binds, remove it and drill a larger pilot hole. Candle wax will help the screw to penetrate.

DON'T start putting in a screw without making a pilot hole first.

BEWARE

Poor quality screwdrivers are often coated to make them look better than they really are. The real test is the hardness of the blade which in poor quality tools may be nowhere near sufficient. Always buy reputable brands, even if they seem a little more expensive.

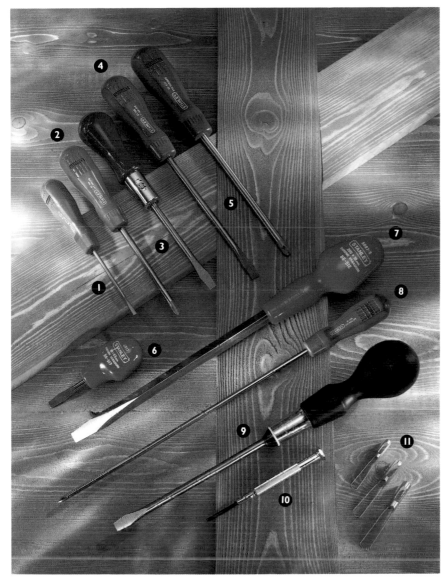

I	Parallel tip screwdriver	**4**	Flared tip screwdriver	**7**	Square bar screwdriver	**10** Precision instrument screwdriver
2	Phillips screwdriver	**5**	Supadriv/Posidriv screwdriver	**8**	Long reach screwdriver	**11** Attachments for holding screws on screwdriver tips
3	Ratchet screwdriver	**6**	Stubby screwdriver	**9**	Wooden cabinet handle screwdriver	

OTHER SCREWDRIVERS

There is often a need to put screws into awkward or tight places. Here are some you could choose:

YANKEE RATCHET

Can be used either as a normal fixed shank screwdriver or, with the ratchet fully working, it allows you to tighten or untighten a screw without having to turn the handle in your hand. It drives screws in much faster than a conventional screwdriver. Pump action screwdrivers, such as the Yankee spiral ratchet, are ideal for repetitive work in softwoods.

STUBBY

Very short, often available with a chunky handle to give good leverage in very tight spaces.

LONG REACH

Made extra long so that you can work in an otherwise restricted part of a construction.

OFFSET (CRANKED)

Set at 90 degrees so that you can reach very confined areas. Invaluable at times.

Yankee spiral ratchet screwdriver

PRECISION HEAD

Not often used for woodwork but available in a range of extremely small tip sizes. Ideal for clock, watch and eyeglasses repairs. The end of the handle rotates and fits into the palm of your hand allowing you to turn the screwdriver with your fingers.

SHANKS AND TIPS The shank and tip of a screwdriver determine the type of job to which it is best suited:

ROUND SHANK Generally more suited to working in wood.

SQUARE SHANK Not generally used for woodwork. Made from square-section steel. A wrench can be used with it to give extra leverage.

FLARED TIP Usually forged and then precision ground, providing much more strength than a parallel tip.

PARALLEL TIP Usually produced in conjunction with round shank and intended to be used for lighter work, including electronics.

PHILLIPS OR CROSSPOINT See Technical Talk, page 51.

Flared tip

Parallel tip

Crosspoint

SCREWS

Screws are used to fasten one material to another.
The type to use depends on the thread of the screw, the head,
the materials being joined and the screw size. Some
screws look more attractive than others and you may want to
consider this too.

All these factors will determine which screw is the best one to use for any particular job. For example, if you are making top quality original or reproduction furniture, the best choice would be steel or brass, slotted, countersunk, wood screws. If all the slots are made to point in the same direction, this can look even more stylish.

On the other hand, you may be working in chipboard, where both the material and aesthetic concerns are different. In this case it might be wiser to use a Phillips screw with a twin thread which is designed for fastening sheet materials. It sounds complicated, but you will understand more as we look at the various types.

HEAD SHAPE AND TYPE

Raised head | Countersunk or flat head | Round head | Slotted head | Phillips head

RAISED HEAD Generally used to fasten handles and fittings to woodwork. The hole must be countersunk as with flat-headed screws.

COUNTERSUNK OR FLAT HEAD This is the traditional wood screw head. The clearance hole will need to be countersunk (using a countersink bit – see page 45), allowing the top of the screw to sit flush with or, alternatively, slightly below the surface of the wood.

ROUND HEAD The shoulder of the screw lies flush with the surface of the fitting. Often used to secure furniture

hardware where it is impractical to use countersink heads.

SLOTTED HEAD Has a simple slot across the screw head, into which the blade of the screwdriver fits.

PHILLIPS HEAD Designed to prevent slipping and therefore damage of the workpiece. Phillips heads will not withstand the same amount of leverage as slotted ones. Sometimes the head is adapted slightly to permit the use of both slotted and Phillips screwdrivers. There are several less common crosspoint head brand names.

SCREWDRIVERS

Screw size		Size of screwdriver tip to be used	
gauge #	screw width (in)	tip width (in)	cross point size
2	.086	⅛	1
4	.112	⁵⁄₃₂	1
6	.138	³⁄₁₆	2
8	.164	¼	2
10	.190	⁵⁄₁₆	2
12	.216	⅜	3

THE THREAD

TRADITIONAL WOOD SCREW Used to fasten softwoods, hardwoods and plywoods, especially in traditional cabinet work and general woodwork.

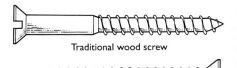

Traditional wood screw

Twin thread wood screw

TWIN THREAD Very high pulling power. Especially suitable for fastening man-made sheet materials as the grip is much stronger than a traditional wood screw.

HOW TO PUT IN A WOOD SCREW

Following a few simple procedures will ensure that any pieces of wood you screw together end up exactly where you need them.

First select the size and type of wood screw you need (see page 50) and mark on the wood exactly where the screw holes should be. Use a marking gauge and try square to put a small cross in the correct position. You should use either a sharp pencil or a knife to make the cross.

Next, drill a small pilot hole through both pieces of wood to be joined, going in slightly less than the full length of the screw. Clamp the pieces together to hold them in place if necessary. This pilot hole should be slightly smaller than the thread size of

the screw and will allow the screw to bite into the wood without splitting it. Softwoods, such as pine, usually need a slightly smaller pilot hole than tough hardwoods such as oak.

You now have a hole marking the screw's corresponding position on each piece of wood. Select a second drill bit, either the same size as the gauge of the screws or very slightly larger, and drill through the top piece of wood only. This is the clearance hole and the screw will fit through it.

If the hole needs countersinking use a countersink bit next, but again be careful not to drill too deeply. Now drive in the wood screw, and you will find that the two pieces of wood will be held perfectly in place.

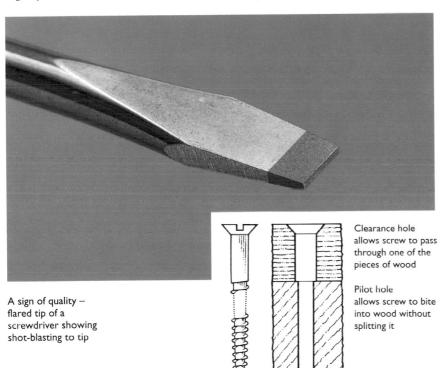

A sign of quality – flared tip of a screwdriver showing shot-blasting to tip

Clearance hole allows screw to pass through one of the pieces of wood

Pilot hole allows screw to bite into wood without splitting it

BRASS SCREWS

Brass is very soft, so where brass screws are to be used on cabinet work it is essential that after you have drilled the pilot and clearance holes, you drive a steel screw of the same size and gauge into the screw hole first, and then

remove it. If you do this, there is much less chance when you fit the brass screw of it becoming damaged or breaking off at the screw head. Never attempt to force a brass screw into place.

TOOLS USED FOR HOLDING

When you are working with wood, there are two main reasons for
holding it steady. The first is to allow maximum control during cutting; the second,
to keep the wood in position while gluing up. There are several
tools for holding wood.

1 C-clamp
2 Woodworker's
bench vise
3 T-bar sash clamp
4 Flat bar sash clamp
5 Clamp heads
6 Fast screw clamp

HOW TO USE CLAMPS

SHORT CLAMPS

These are used to hold smaller pieces of work or to steady them while cutting. There are several types:

BENCH HOLDFAST Used to hold wood when cutting out joints. Fits through a previously drilled hole in the workbench top.

C-CLAMP A small general purpose clamp varying in capacity from 1in (25mm) to 12in (300mm). So-called because it resembles the letter C.

QUICK-CLAMP Also known as a fast clamp or speed clamp, this is similar to a C-clamp, but slides more easily to length before being screwed up tight, making adjustments much faster than with a C-clamp. So-called because when loosened the head slides freely on the bar.

LONG CLAMPS

Long clamps are used for gluing up frames, tops and carcase constructions.

BAR CLAMPS Essentially a long steel bar with a tail slide at one end and a movable head at the other. They are used in the gluing up of frames and carcases. The bar clamp is a simple concept, and an invaluable tool.

The best quality bar clamps are known as T-bar clamps, so-named because they have a T-shaped steel bar, for extra strength. They do not bend when tightened and are heavy clamps to handle.

The flat bar type of bar clamp is more suitable for much lighter work and is the most usual one for home woodworking. You can use extension pieces to increase the length of both T-bar and flat bar clamps.

SPECIALIZED CLAMPS There is a multitude of unusual clamps – miter clamps, flooring clamps, edge clamps, fret clamps, double ended clamps, quick grip clamps.... One thing is for sure, you should be able to find something that will do the job.

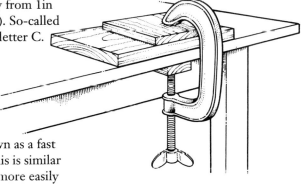

Always protect the workpiece and the workbench with a protective block

Another option is to buy separate clamp heads, for which you supply your own piece of wood or iron pipe for the bar. With these you decide yourself what the length of the clamp will be. Either beech or maple is suitable for wooden bars; for pipe clamps, use ¾in black iron pipe, not galvanized.

There is also available a much longer version of the short quick-clamp, which allows for very rapid setting up while gluing.

See page 86 for more on using sash clamps and keeping frames square.

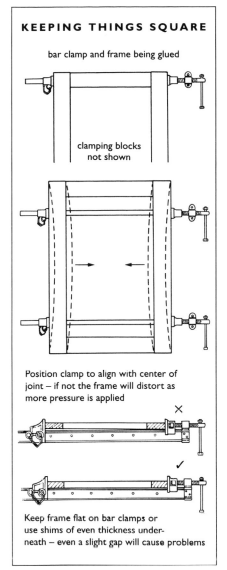

See page 86 for more on using sash clamps and keeping frames square.

KEEPING THINGS SQUARE

bar clamp and frame being glued

clamping blocks not shown

Position clamp to align with center of joint – if not the frame will distort as more pressure is applied

Keep frame flat on bar clamps or use shims of even thickness underneath – even a slight gap will cause problems

IMPORTANT

Make sure you take time and care when using bar clamps. Always ensure they are in the correct position as components dry. You have only one opportunity to get it right.

GOOD HABITS

Place the head and tail slide of a bar clamp in line with the joint when gluing up, or the stile or rail of a frame will bend as you tighten up and you will not be able to check it for being square.

Always protect the workpiece with wooden blocks.

Do not let frames, or boards being joined edge to edge, become bowed as a result of being held incorrectly. If there is a small amount of movement when you are clamping up, either fasten on another clamp (this time on top of the boards) to balance out the stresses or use cauls to flatten out the boards.

THE VISE

The two single most important tools used in woodwork are the bench and the vise. There are two main sorts of vise: the engineer's vise, which has steel jaws, but stands above the bench top, making it unsuitable for wood-work; and the woodworker's vise. A woodworker's vise has wooden protective pieces which you attach to the jaws to avoid damaging the workpiece. The jaws lie flat and in line with the bench top, allowing you to work, unrestricted, on frames and panels.

The quality of the vise is very important. Always ensure it is well made. It is convenient to have a quick-release mechanism, which allows you to open the jaws to their maximum capacity quickly and easily. It also enables you to close the vise without having to wind it in laboriously.

One word of warning – a vise is designed for holding objects firmly in its jaws, so that you can mark out and cut joints. It is not designed to have whatever it is holding hit with a hammer. This will either damage the screw mechanism or dislodge the screws holding the vise to the bench. Vises are an expensive one-time purchase; if you buy the right one, it will be money well spent, but do not treat it badly.

TIP

Never ever hold metal objects in a woodworker's vise as this will immediately damage the wooden jaws of the vise.

HOW TO FIT A WOODWORKER'S VISE

1 Fit the wooden jaws to the vise first. The jaws should be made from a dense hardwood, such as beech or maple, and should be between ⅝in (15mm) and ¾in (20mm) thick. Ensure the tops of the jaws are planed flat and level.

2 Turn the bench upside down on a flat surface and rest the vise (also upside down) on the same surface. This will show you the thickness of the shims you require.

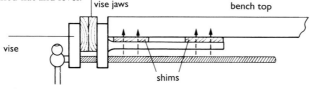

3 Insert the shims. Mark and drill the pilot and clearance holes for fixing the screws. Use lag screws, machine screws or carriage bolts to fit the vise.

4 Next turn the bench the correct way up. Make sure that the jaws are level with the bench top. Use either a hand plane or adjust the shims if necessary.

CABINET MAKER'S WOODEN BENCH VISE

Unlike the woodworker's vise (shown) which generally stands proud of the front of the bench and is mostly made of metal, the cabinet maker's bench vise is a wooden vise having the edge of the bench top as one of its jaws, the other jaw pulling up against it. The advantage is that you are able to hold pieces of wood parallel and right up to the edge of the bench. The disadvantage is that one of the jaws is actually the bench top. If it becomes damaged, the repair will be very difficult and expensive.

BENCH STOP

A bench stop is a small square block of wood (the stop) fitted to a metal slide which is fastened underneath the bench. This allows it to be raised or lowered through a square hole in the bench top.

WHY USE ONE?

Sometimes woodworkers will try to plane wood to size in a vise. This has two major disadvantages:

• When planing wider boards, a vise is often not wide enough to take the wood, or distorts it as the vise is wound in.

• When planing lengths of wood longer than the vise jaws the ends are unsupported. It is impossible in this situation to make wood flat with a hand plane as its weight will cause the wood to bend.

The second point is the most important one and many woodworkers blame themselves for not being able to produce straight edges. The problem is exacerbated when planing small dimensions. In this case it is therefore essential to use the bench as a supporting flat base, planing up against a bench stop. A vise should only be used to hold wide pieces such as table tops when planing edges.

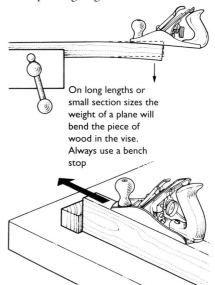

On long lengths or small section sizes the weight of a plane will bend the piece of wood in the vise. Always use a bench stop

HOLDING AWKWARD SHAPES

If you watch a plumber bend copper tubing, you soon realize that to do it properly you need special tools. This rule also applies to holding and gluing awkward shapes. The only way to achieve a professional result is to think ahead, which means designing and assembling your project so that either you do not have any awkward shapes to hold in the first place, or, if you do, a jig or extra clamp is available to put pressure exactly where you need it. It could easily take you longer to make the jig than to do the job of gluing up.

If the work you are doing involves a particularly awkward shape, such as gluing up a chair, you will usually find there is a special clamp or tool made for the job. If you need to put extra pressure at one specific point, you can quite easily rig up a quick clamp yourself, such as a loop of rope with a stick threaded through to tighten it (a Spanish windlass).

> **TIP**
>
> If you need to stop a small part from popping out of position during gluing, try using a small weight or drafting tape to hold it in place as it dries.

1 Web clamp
2 Frame clamp

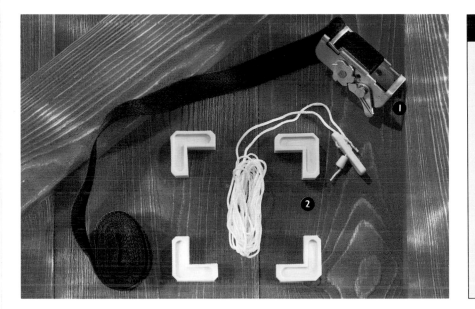

> ### TECHNICAL TALK
>
> **CAULS** As used here, a length of wood curved on one face only and used in conjunction with a pair of C-clamps, which will deliver firm pressure to the center of a board, pushing it flat.
>
> **HEAD & TAIL SLIDE** The head of a bar clamp is fastened to an adjustable screw thread, whereas the tail slide moves freely along the bar and is secured by means of a steel pin. The tail slide is set to a suitable length for the job before the head of the clamp is tightened.

HOLDING MITERED FRAMES

There are many ways of holding mitered frames together, some involving quite sophisticated clamps. One of the easiest methods is to use a frame clamp. These are ideal for small to medium frames but not so good for larger ones.

1 Cut the miters and make sure that each pair of lengths making up the frame is exactly the same by putting the pieces back-to-back. Clean up the joints.

2 When gluing up, set the frame clamp to approximately the right size. Put three of the sides of the frame into the clamp. Inserting the fourth side of the picture frame should put a slight stress on the frame clamp, which will gently hold the frame in position. Tighten the clamp fully. It is important to keep the frame flat on a base board and only gently push the fourth side into place.

3 After tightening the clamp, check for square and adjust if necessary.

> **TIP**
>
> Cut the longest lengths first, then if you make a mistake you can use these for the shorter ones.

> ### SHOPPING GUIDE
>
> **ESSENTIAL TOOLS**
>
> **C-CLAMPS 3IN (75MM) AND 4IN (100MM)** Varied uses; 6in (150mm) is also a handy addition to the tool kit.
>
> **BAR CLAMPS** Size depends on the type of work. Well engineered flat bar clamps, either 36in (900mm) or 48in (1200mm) long, are the most useful.
>
> **WOODWORKER'S VISE** Preferably with a quick release mechanism. The Record No 53 is a particularly good vise, able to extend to 15in (380mm).

CARING FOR YOUR TOOLS

SHARPENING

The best plane or chisel in the world is useless without a sharp cutting edge. Plane blades should, in fact, be so sharp that you could cut human hair with them. An old workshop test was actually to shave hair from the lower forearm with a plane blade. The best ways of improving the quality of your woodworking are to concentrate on the techniques of accurate layout, to prepare fine cutting edges on your tools and to practise the techniques until you get them right. You cannot only half-sharpen tools and expect them to work correctly – they won't.

SHARPENING PLANE BLADES

When a plane blade is made it is hardened and ground by the manufacturer. The final cutting edge is produced by you, not by the factory. When you acquire the blade, it may not be absolutely flat. Therefore it will need to be 'backed off' on a sharpening stone.

The cutting edge of the blade is formed by honing (sharpening) at a slightly steeper angle than the grinding angle, (usually 25 degrees). The best angle at which to hone is approximately 30 degrees. This figure is really an ideal, and as long as you do not make the honing angle too steep or too shallow, you will still be able to achieve a good fine edge. If you are not confident about holding the blade at the correct angle, you may prefer to use a honing guide which will hold the blade steady for you (see page 33).

Sharpening a plane blade (backing off)

Honing a plane blade

HOW TO SHARPEN

I use an oil stone to sharpen plane blades and chisels. Put a little light machine oil on the surface of the stone and spread it around with your finger. To produce the cutting edge itself, back off the blade to flatten it, and then hone the front bevel. Backing off the blade will allow the cap iron of the plane to lie perfectly flat on it.

BACKING OFF

Put the back of the plane blade on a fine oil stone and push it backward and forward using firm pressure. Always keep the blade totally flat against the surface. When it has been backed off completely you will have flattened the full width of the blade at its cutting edge. The steel should appear bright and shiny.

HONING

The next stage is to sharpen the bevel of the plane blade. Put the bevel on the stone's surface and feel where it actually 'sits' on the stone. Then lift the blade up slightly (about 5 degrees) to produce the honing angle. Move the blade backward and forward covering the whole surface of the stone (especially the ends of it, which will help to keep the stone flatter). Do not allow the blade to rock as you move it around. The honed edge will soon be seen as a thin, shiny (polished) line at the cutting edge of the blade.

WHAT NEXT?

Keep sharpening until you have backed off the blade and honed it too. It is usual to alternate between the two as this makes the whole process less boring. A fine 'wire edge' should form at the cutting edge to give you an indication that you are nearly there. It should take roughly 20 to 30 minutes to sharpen a completely new blade, but much less for one that has previously been backed off and honed. After the honing process the blade can be stropped to produce an even sharper cutting edge (see page 58).

HOW TO SHARPEN THE PLANE BLADE

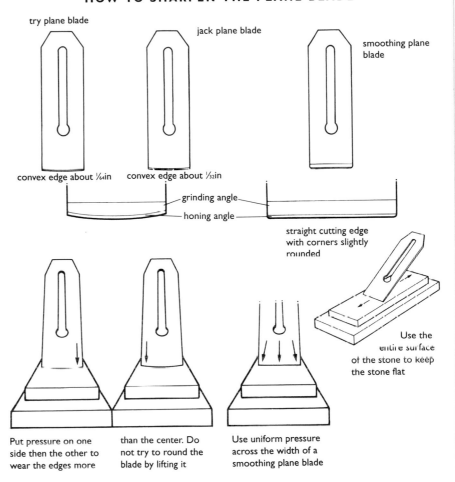

try plane blade

jack plane blade

smoothing plane blade

convex edge about ¼in   convex edge about ⅟₃₂in

grinding angle
honing angle

straight cutting edge with corners slightly rounded

Use the entire surface of the stone to keep the stone flat

Put pressure on one side then the other to wear the edges more

than the center. Do not try to round the blade by lifting it

Use uniform pressure across the width of a smoothing plane blade

25°

Grinding angle
angle at which the blade has been ground at the factory ready for sharpening

30°

Honing angle
slightly more than the grinding angle, this is the actual cutting edge of a blade

CONVEX EDGE Jack, try and fore planes have a convex cutting edge put on their blades rather than a straight one. To produce a convex edge, simply put more pressure on the outside edges of the blade as you sharpen it. This wears it more on the edges, to form a slightly rounded edge. Do not try to lift the blade or to round it deliberately as the corners will dig in and damage the stone.

STRAIGHT EDGE If you are sharpening a smoothing plane blade, which has a straight cutting edge, keep the pressure uniform across the blade and sharpening stone (ensure that the stone is flat). The corners can be slightly rounded later by lightly stroking them against the edge of the sharpening stone. This will stop the plane blade from digging into the surface of the wood during use.

SHARPENING CHISELS

The rules for sharpening plane blades apply to chisels too. You will have to back off and hone the chisel on a sharpening stone, ensuring that the cutting edge remains uniformly flat and checking that you do not rock the blade as you push it backward and forward. When sharpening a very narrow blade ¼in (6mm) or less there is a great risk that the chisel will wobble from side to side. The best technique is to sharpen it by positioning the chisel at right angles to the stone (see below). Use the side of the stone as a guide for your hands, pushing the chisel backward and forward along the stone, but be careful not to remove the skin from your fingers as you work.

Wider chisels can be sharpened by moving the chisel along the length of the stone in long ovals, circles or figure-eight movements. Always keep the chisel at the correct angle. Don't concentrate on just one particular area of the stone as it will wear unevenly.

When the wire edge appears, as with plane blades, you are well on the way to achieving a good cutting edge. If you achieve a wire edge and the chisel will not cut correctly, the chisel is either made from a steel which is not hard enough to sharpen or you are honing the blade at too high an angle.

After honing, strop the blade on leather, using firm pressure (see below). Always pull the chisel toward you to protect the strop from damage. It is a good idea to use one strop for chisels and one for plane blades, because narrower chisels tend to create grooves in the face of the strop.

You can safely test the sharpness of a chisel edge by paring the end grain of wood, especially that of a hard or tough wood. If it cuts cleanly, then the chisel is sharp.

3 Backing off a chisel blade

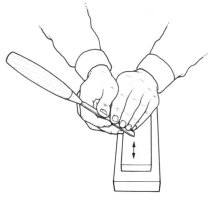
2 Narrow chisels can be controlled by pushing them backward and forward at 90 degrees to the edge. Steady the blade by using the side of the stone as a guide

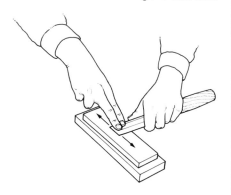

1 Use figure-eight movements, circles or long ovals to hone the edge of the chisel. Cover the entire surface of the sharpening stone to keep it flat

HOW TO USE A LEATHER STROP

After honing a chisel or plane blade, the next stage is to strop it up, a bit like a barber using leather to sharpen a cut-throat razor. The process is simple. Place the blade on the strop at the same angle as its newly honed edge and draw it back toward you using heavy pressure. After six or so strokes, turn the blade on its back and again draw it toward you, this time flat against the strop, and again using firm pressure. By pulling the blade toward you rather than pushing away there is no chance of accidentally damaging or tearing the strop. Repeat this process three or four times. If you have honed the edge correctly, stropping will produce a blade as keen as a razor blade, so be careful.

firm pressure here ↓

plane blade

strop

Use firm pressure to increase the sharpness of a honed blade.

plywood baseboard

WHAT TO USE TO MAKE A STROP

You could use straightforward ⅛–¼in (4–6mm) thick leather with a good face, or, even better, chrome leather, which is pale blue in color. A little oil will help lubricate it in use. You can buy ready-made strops, which may work better if you use stropping paste, Carborundum powder or some other fine, powdered abrasive to speed up the cutting action. Once you have acquired the habit of using a strop regularly for sharpening tools, you will be amazed at how quickly the quality of your woodworking improves.

THE SHARPENING STONE

Sharpening stones are either natural or synthetic. The best quality, but unfortunately most expensive, natural stones are Arkansas stones, which are available in three grades. These are known as soft (coarse), hard (medium) and black hard (fine). Synthetic stones are classed as coarse, medium or fine or are available as a combination stone, which contains two different grades of stone, bonded back-to-back. Natural and synthetic stones rely on oil as the lubricant. A third type, the Japanese water stone, uses water, as its name suggests. A range of diamond stones is also available. These are useful for sharpening tungsten carbide router bits, as well as chisels and plane blades.

LUBRICATING SHARPENING STONES

For oil stones, use light engineering oil as the lubricant. For water stones, always soak a stone in water before its initial use and never let it freeze as this will cause it to crack. Diamond stones may be lubricated with water or oil.

DO'S AND DONT'S

DO keep the stone flat by moving tools around the face of the stone as you sharpen them

DON'T let the stone rock or move around while sharpening

DO keep the stone clean of dirt and grime

DON'T let the cutting edges of tools dig in and damage the stone

DO use plenty of pressure while sharpening

TIP

Do not use motor oil or heavy engineering oil for lubricating oil stones. A light engineering oil will protect both the stone and the tool being sharpened.

LOOKING AFTER YOUR TOOLS

- Always protect the blade of a bench plane by keeping the plane on its side when not in use. Never use the lever cap to separate the cap iron and plane blade.
- Never leave hand tools in a damp atmosphere. Preferably, protect with oiled paper.
- Protect chisel and saw blades from damage by using blade covers.
- Never use a cutting edge that is not sharp. This is both dangerous and will damage the work, and maybe the tool itself.
- Do not use top quality tools on recycled wood or over nail heads. Never remove paint with a bench plane or cabinet scraper.
- Always re-grind (or have someone else re-grind) plane and chisel blades when honing has removed most of the original grinding edge.

TECHNICAL TALK

HONING The final sharpening which produces the cutting edge. Tools can be re-honed as they blunt as long as there is a ground angle left at the end of the plane blade or chisel.

SHOPPING GUIDE

ESSENTIAL TOOLS

FINE OR FINE/MEDIUM SYNTHETIC OIL STONE The combination stone gives you two grades, back-to-back.

SUGGESTED ADDITIONAL TOOLS

FINE NATURAL SHARPENING STONE A very expensive luxury, but the quality is superb.

LEATHER STROP Either buy one or alternatively you can make one yourself (see opposite).

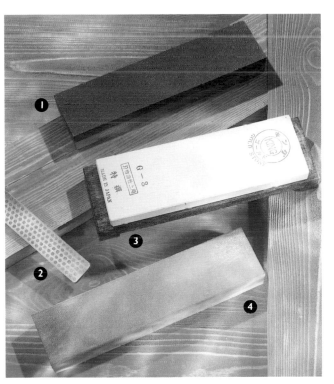

1 Combination oil stone
2 Diamond sharpening stone
3 Japanese water stone
4 Natural sharpening stone

Techniques

Now that you have a kit of basic tools, and know how to use them, it's time to learn the techniques you need to be able to make a piece of furniture. The pages in this section will take you through the whole process of layout; planing the wood to make it flat, square, and of uniform thickness; cutting and fitting all kinds of joints, from simple butt joints to more complex dovetails; assembling the pieces of wood and gluing them together; and cleaning up, sanding and finishing.

Work through this section logically: it is worth getting each technique right before you move on to the next. The illustrations are designed to make each technique as clear as possible, and once again there are plenty of tips and technical talk boxes to help you along.

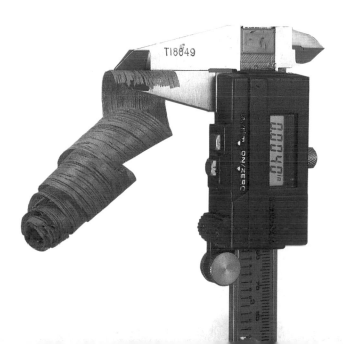

LAYOUT

No matter how much you practice, the fit of a joint can only be
as good as the care you take at the layout stage. If you are measuring where a joint
should be, never just guess – instead, make sure that it
is in the right place. The golden rule is – think twice, cut once.

Always work logically following a sequence that makes certain you know where each part goes. Numbering each joint as you progress will help you avoid making mistakes.

FACE SIDE AND FACE EDGE MARKS

Once you have selected one face of a piece of wood for its appearance and planed it true and flat, see page 66, always mark it as shown for ease of identification. This is a face side mark. Next, when you have made a square edge by working from the face side, mark this with the face edge mark. When you have marked the face side and face edge, the wood can be gauged to width, planed and then gauged to thickness.

Used properly, face side and edge marks tell you the best face and edge, identify a square corner from which to gauge joints, and allow you to lay out perfect shoulder lines.

face side mark

face edge mark

Mark face side first, then face edge. Next gauge to width. Plane and gauge to thickness

TIP
If you have many shoulder lines to mark (see opposite) you can hold all the pieces in a vise and lay them out together. Again use the first piece as a template but be careful that the layout lines are all at exactly 90 degrees: even the slightest discrepancy will mean that the shoulder lines will not match each other.

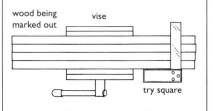

wood being marked out

vise

try square

TIP
Start each line by putting the point of the knife or pencil actually on the previous knife line; then move the square up to it.

HOW TO LAY OUT A SHOULDER LINE

You will need a try square, a marking knife and a pencil. Work from the face side and face edge to produce a perfect line to saw to.

1 Mark on the face side and face edge. If you feel unsure about using a knife to mark shoulders, use a sharp pencil first, and then go over the lines accurately with the knife. Using the try square, work from the face edge and mark a shoulder line on the face side.
2 From the face side, mark a line across the face edge.
3 From the face side, mark a knife line on the edge opposite the face edge.
4 Finally, from the face edge, join up the lines to make a perfect shoulder all around the four surfaces. **Always work the stock of the square from the face side or face edge marks**.

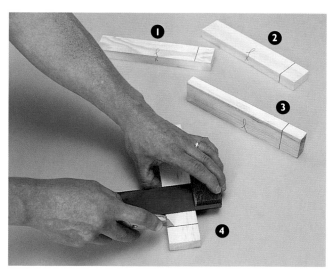

REMEMBER
• Decide what measurements are needed before you start laying out any of the pieces – don't forget to allow for joints.
• For accuracy, use a knife for lines that are to be sawn/chiselled to.
• Use a pencil to mark face side/face edge marks, waste, and any other notes.

THE BEGINNINGS OF A CABINET

Basic cabinet making may involve making a simple framework, perhaps a door frame intended to fit exactly into an opening. The frame cannot be bigger or smaller than the opening: where do you start?

Measure accurately the internal dimensions of the door opening. Ensure that it is square – if not, allow for any extra and add it to the width.

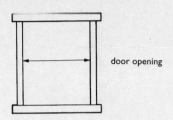

door opening

Measure the width of the stiles and deduct these from the width of the door opening. This will give you the exact length required for the shoulders. Do not forget to allow extra for the joints.

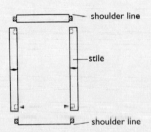

shoulder line

stile

shoulder line

Lay out and cut the shoulder lines accurately. When the joints have been fitted, the door should fit the opening. It is wise to allow for a little more than the opening on the width – say ½in (1–2mm) – to allow for planing to an exact fit later.

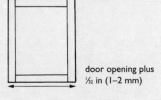

door opening plus ½ in (1–2 mm)

Make up a frame with all the face sides pointing toward you, and the face edges pointing inward, to guarantee that the joints will match each other. Here the face side marks show the outside of the door – i.e. what you see

MAKING SHOULDER LINES MATCH EACH OTHER

Locating a single shoulder line is simple enough, but what about making up a series of shoulder lines all of which have to match each other, perhaps for a set of bookcase shelves, or maybe rails that will make up the carcase of a piece of furniture?

These are the stages of exactly copying the shoulders on one piece of wood to one or more other pieces. Assume in this case that two tenons, ¾in (19mm) long, are to be put on the ends of the rails. Allow for these in the measuring, so that you do not start off with a length of wood that will in the end be too short for the job.

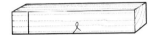

1 Mark the first shoulder line from the face edge, allowing more than you need for the tenon.

2 Use a steel rule in order to lay out the exact position of the second shoulder, using the end of the knife.

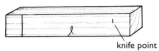

knife point

3 Remove the rule and put the knife point back into the mark it has made.

waste

4 Slide the square up to the knife with the stock of the square on the face edge. Knife the second shoulder. Use a pencil to establish the length of the tenons. Label the waste.

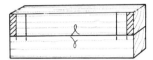

5 Bring the second piece up to the first, marking the position of the shoulders with the end of the knife. Repeat for the other pieces.

6 On each piece use a square to lay out two new shoulder lines. Use a square and knife to continue the shoulders around all four sides (see page 62).

HOW TO USE A MARKING GAUGE

A marking gauge is a simple tool but it takes a little practice to use one properly. Having a point (or two points in the case of a mortise gauge), it is designed to scribe an accurate line along a face or edge. A marking gauge gives a definite groove to work to as it actually scores the wood. If you are marking across the grain, use a cutting gauge, not a marking gauge. This has a blade which will actually cut the fibers instead of tearing them out. Cutting gauges are used to lay out the shoulders of housing joints.

The two points on a mortise gauge allow you to scribe two parallel lines on the wood simultaneously, at a measured distance from the edge. This gauge is most often used to mark the positions of mortise and tenon joints. The distance between the two pins is easy to adjust; it is usual for this to be the width of the chisel you will use to cut the mortise.

LAYOUT

Always work from the face side or face edge to ensure that the joints correspond to each other after cutting.

Hold the gauge in your right hand to give maximum control. Keep the piece of wood being gauged at an angle of 30–45 degrees, either pushing it against a bench stop or holding it securely in a vise. Work the gauge away from you while using light pressure to push against the edge of the wood with the stock. This will help keep it parallel to the edge and stop the point following the grain.

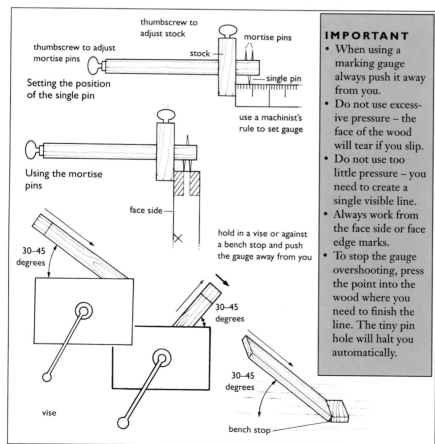

thumbscrew to adjust stock

thumbscrew to adjust mortise pins

stock

mortise pins

single pin

Setting the position of the single pin

use a machinist's rule to set gauge

Using the mortise pins

face side

hold in a vise or against a bench stop and push the gauge away from you

30–45 degrees

30–45 degrees

30–45 degrees

vise

bench stop

IMPORTANT
- When using a marking gauge always push it away from you.
- Do not use excessive pressure – the face of the wood will tear if you slip.
- Do not use too little pressure – you need to create a single visible line.
- Always work from the face side or face edge marks.
- To stop the gauge overshooting, press the point into the wood where you need to finish the line. The tiny pin hole will halt you automatically.

SETTING THE DISTANCE FROM THE PIN TO THE STOCK

Untighten the thumbscrew on the stock slightly and use a steel rule to measure the exact distance needed between this and the center of the pin. Hold the stock (which would otherwise move) in your left hand to control it. Tighten the thumbscrew slightly and check the measurement again. If you need to make a slight adjustment, gently tap one or other end to move the stock a fraction. When you are satisfied that you have set the gauge correctly, firmly tighten the thumbscrew and double check the measurement.

THE RIGHT JOINTS FOR THE JOB

You will find specific details on how to lay out, cut and fit important joints
on pages 72–82. Whether you are putting up a shelf or working on advanced cabinet making,
it is vital to choose the right joint at the outset: decide on the type of joint
before cutting the wood to length, ready for laying out.

Most joints, when correctly cut and glued, are strong. If used for the wrong application though (e.g. dowel joints to secure a drawer front) they will soon become weak and fail. Always choose a joint that offers sufficient strength or resistance to pulling or pushing if this is important.

Some joints are easy to lay out and cut, others more difficult. As a rule, the more complex the joint, the stronger it generally is.

1 Bridle joint
2 Stopped, barefaced dado joint
3 Half-lap joint
4 Mortise and tenon joint
5 Dovetail joint

Correctly laid out joints with the waste clearly shown ready for removal

EASY JOINTS

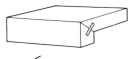

DOWEL JOINT Two pieces of wood held together with long pegs (dowels). The grain runs along the length of the dowel. Offers no resistance to pulling

MITER JOINT A simple joint for corners, usually at 90 degrees. Can be strengthened with glue blocks

LAP JOINT OR RABBET JOINT A corner joint; one piece covers the other for a more attractive detail than a simple butt joint

MITER JOINT WITH LOOSE TONGUE A strengthened mitered joint relying on an inserted piece of wood for extra support

BUTT JOINT Two pieces of wood simply glued together. Two major types: edge-to-edge and corner butt joints. Can be strengthened by using loose tongues or glue blocks

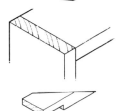

HALF-LAP JOINT Two pieces of wood, with equal amounts cut from each; when interlocked, the overall thickness of the joint equals the amount of wood removed

MORE DIFFICULT JOINTS

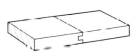

TONGUE AND GROOVE JOINT An edge joint where the tongue on one piece fits into a groove on the other. Sometimes used in panelling or tops, and flooring to allow for shrinkage

DADO JOINT A traditional joint often used in bookcases to fasten a shelf to the sides. Main types are through, stepped (barefaced) and dovetail

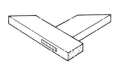

MORTISE AND TENON Most commonly used traditional joint. Very strong, relying on a tight fit for strength. Used for frame and carcase constructions. Through mortise shown

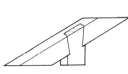

DOVETAILED LAP JOINT A lap joint with dovetail wedge, producing a very strong shoulder. If pulled, it will tighten itself. A very good frame joint

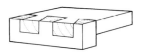

THROUGH DOVETAIL JOINT Wedge-shaped extensions interlock like fingers. Very strong but time consuming to cut and fit

HALF-BLIND DOVETAIL JOINT Dovetail joint where one half extends and covers over the other piece. Used for traditional drawer fronts

PLANING

Although the days of laboriously having to hand plane each
and every piece of wood have gone, this does not mean to say that bench planes have
been superseded by machines.

Machines are capable of planing vast quantities of wood. This means that they cannot be selective, and planing machines regularly produce defects such as torn grain and cutter marks. This, combined with the fact that most do not guarantee that planed wood will be produced straight and true, means that in terms of quality, bench planes are easily able to out-class their larger and more powerful relatives.

Correctly used, bench planes will smooth and flatten wood and will remove most of the defects that machines cause. On the finest quality work, once the wood has been planed by machine, each and every piece should really also be planed by hand.

HOW TO PLANE BOARDS FLAT

Wood is a totally natural material that responds to changes in the moisture content of the atmosphere by either expanding or contracting (see page 11). Therefore, wood may well warp or distort in some way as it re-adjusts to new surroundings. If this movement occurs after the wood has been allowed to stabilize by secondary conditioning (see page 12), bench planes are used to flatten the surface of the wood, to prepare it for joining and sanding.

4 Start by planing the high areas, taking these down to finish, eventually, at the lowest point. Do not put more cut on the plane to try to speed up the process as it will simply dig into the wood.

5 Work the whole surface of the board, either along its length or at an angle from its edges (traversing – see illustration right). You can work straight across the face if you want to but if you do, take extra care.

6 Try to avoid creating too much torn grain as you work and keep checking to see how much of the surface has been flattened. Finish off along the board's length.

THE PROCESS

Ensure that your workbench top is flat before you start.

1 Place the board to be planed flat on the workbench. It may have already been planed by machine at this stage. Check to see whether it rocks, and if it does (it probably will), put slips of paper or shims underneath the corners to level the board and make it artificially flat.

2 Next, look at the board to check for any high or low areas, so that you can clearly visualize which parts of the surface need to be worked first.

3 Select either a jack or fore plane that is sharpened and correctly set up for planing boards flat (see page 57).

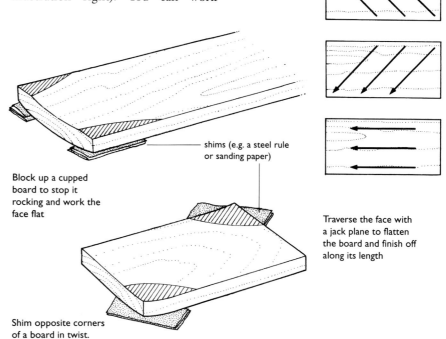

shims (e.g. a steel rule or sanding paper)

Block up a cupped board to stop it rocking and work the face flat

Shim opposite corners of a board in twist. Work from the high points towards the lowest

Traverse the face with a jack plane to flatten the board and finish off along its length

Shims under the corners of a board keep it stable while the whole surface is being traversed at around 45 degrees with a jack plane

7 When the face is flat, check it, and make this the face side of the board. You can use winding sticks if necessary to check for twist. Next plane an edge, and when you have checked this for square against the face side, mark it as the face edge.

8 You can now gauge the second edge to width and plane it square to the face side (see page 68 – you can use a panel gauge on very wide boards).

9 Next, gauge to thickness and plane the other side of the board flat, by putting the board face side down on the bench top. There should be no need to use shims if you have planed the face side correctly: simply work to the gauge lines.

Note wood that has been prepared with all four surfaces at exactly 90 degrees to each other is known as PSE – Planed Square Edge – or alternatively PAR – Planed All Round. Where the angles are not all at 90 degrees, then the wood is known only as PAR – Planed All Round.

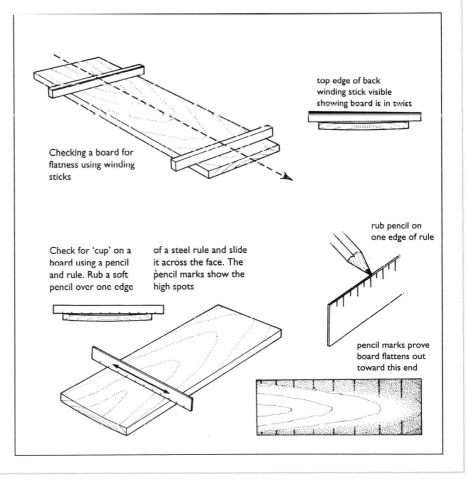

Checking a board for flatness using winding sticks

top edge of back winding stick visible showing board is in twist

Check for 'cup' on a board using a pencil and rule. Rub a soft pencil over one edge of a steel rule and slide it across the face. The pencil marks show the high spots

rub pencil on one edge of rule

pencil marks prove board flattens out toward this end

SQUARING AN EDGE

After planing the face side of a board flat, the next stage is to produce an edge square to it. Narrower pieces of wood are much easier to work with and with a little practice, you will be able to square an edge very quickly and accurately. You can test how you are doing with a try square by putting the stock of the square on the face side and pushing against it. Hold the edge up under a window or in good light to check whether there are any slight gaps – if so, mark them with a pencil.

The illustration on page 69 takes you through the stages of preparing perfectly square edges. You will need a try plane, a try square and a pencil. Note that a correctly sharpened smoothing plane will *not* make edges square.

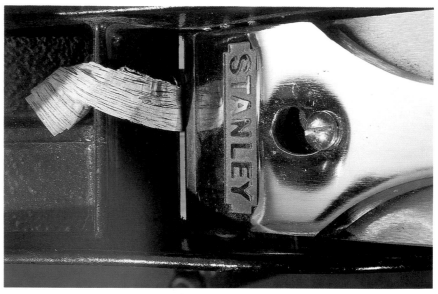

The convex nature of the try plane blade means that by moving the plane from one side of an edge across to the other, an edge will gradually be made square

---

WORKING TO A GAUGED LINE

gauge line

Plane off the bulk of the wood to within ¹⁄₃₂in (1–2mm) using a fore or try plane. Next take off a shaving or two at a time touching the wood where it needs it (see page 69)

feather edge

The penultimate shaving will produce a feather edge (tiny sliver of wood) which will fall off. One more shaving will take you to the center of the gauge line; do not plane beyond this point

---

GOOD ADVICE

• Plane the edge flat along its length first. Next, concentrate on making it square to the face side.

• One of the biggest problems you will face when you first handle a try plane is mastering the technique of pushing forward, while at the same time carefully moving the plane from one side of the edge to the other. The edges become square as you remove the high areas. Your pencil marks (those put on the edge after checking for square) will show you these high spots, and if your technique is correct they will be completely removed after every one or two strokes. This is why you need to keep checking and re-marking the edge with new pencil marks as you go.

• Ten plane shavings measure, on average, about ³⁄₆₄in (1mm) . . . a huge amount of wood! When squaring edges, especially at the final stages, never take off more than two shavings at a time.

PRACTICE YOUR PLANING

A good small project to practice planing edges is to make your own set of winding sticks, which must be perfectly straight (see page 67). These are made from a dry, close-grained hardwood such as beech or maple and should measure around 15in (380mm) long, 1¼in (33mm) wide and ½in (13mm) thick. The back winding stick can be inlaid on its top corner with a dark timber such as American black walnut.

HOW TO PLANE EDGES TO MAKE THEM SQUARE

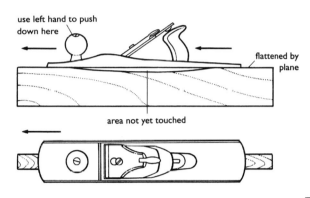

PROBLEMS

edge not straight

edge not square

SOLUTIONS

1 Either plane against a stop or (for edges of wide pieces) put board in a vise. Use a long plane (e.g. a try plane): where the plane touches the edge it will cut; where it does not it will glide over. Don't worry about the edge not being square at this early stage. Always plane from one end to the other

Keep the plane central and keep going until the edge is straight

use left hand to push down here

flattened by plane

area not yet touched

3 Move the plane from one side of the edge to the other as you move forward, hitting the high areas. The edge will eventually be made square. Remove 1-2 shavings at a time. Keep checking for square and add new pencil marks as you go

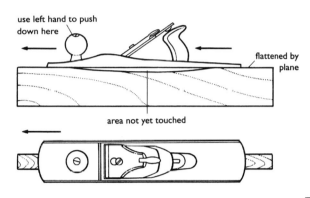

pencil markings (showing the edge is in twist)

keep plane to one side

2 Next make the edge square: test first with a square and mark high spots on the edge clearly in pencil

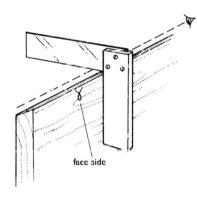

face side

move plane to other side

keep plane on this path to remove third cross

4 Used correctly, the convex try plane blade will create a true edge relative to the face side

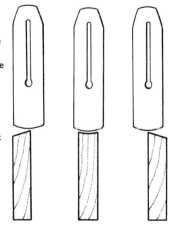

keeping plane to the left removes one side of edge

keeping plane central removes both sides of edge

moving plane to the right removes the other side of edge

5 When the edge is square, finish with one stroke of the plane in a central position

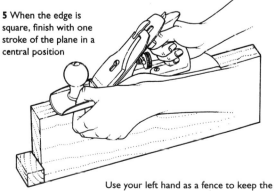

Use your left hand as a fence to keep the plane level as you push forward

PLANING END GRAIN

The end grain of wood requires special attention. Imagine wood as being made up of long fibers standing side by side, like bristles on a brush. Now visualize the brush being upturned: if you were to stroke the bristles with the palm of your hand, the last bristles, being unsupported, would bend over. Fibers of wood behave just like this. Fortunately there are several ways to stop this being a problem.

Whichever method you choose, the main objective when planing end grain is to protect and support the back edge of the wood so it does not tear out. This also applies when paring with a chisel, boring holes or sawing – always support the waste using chopping boards, saw boards or blocks.

> **TIP**
> On wide shelves and panels plane in one direction, then turn the wood in the vise and continue planing in the other direction.

Even though a knife line cuts the fibers of the wood, unless the back edge is properly supported, it will tear out

Method 1
use a plane to square off a stile or rail by working inward. Never allow the wood to be unsupported

Method 2
chamfer off a back corner to give support. Take special care on the final plane strokes

Method 3
use a scrap piece of wood to support the back edge

Method 4
use a shooting board

PLANING SIMPLE DECORATIVE MOLDINGS

Rounds, bevels and chamfers are simple moldings that can be applied to edges to make them look more attractive, or to stop the wood having sharp corners. You can produce them by using special cutters, fitted into a combination plane, or even use an electric router, although the easiest method when preparing only a few decorative edges is the traditional one, using a smoothing plane.

CHAMFERS

A chamfer runs from one face of a piece of wood to the adjacent edge. Mark the position of the chamfer on the appropriate face and edge in pencil. Do not use a marking gauge, because the lines you create will be dif-

ficult to remove. Gauge it by hand instead (see page 22).

After marking, you can start to plane. Use your left hand as a guide to steady the smoothing plane, holding it at the same angle as the chamfer. Work the plane backward and forward until the bulk of the edge has been removed. Double check that you are working to the correct angle: if you are not, adjust the plane accordingly. Work carefully until you reach the pencil gauge lines.

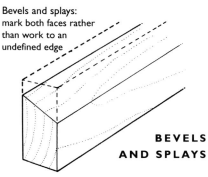

Bevels and splays: mark both faces rather than work to an undefined edge

BEVELS AND SPLAYS

Marking position of chamfer:

use left hand to guide and support plane to produce accurate chamfer

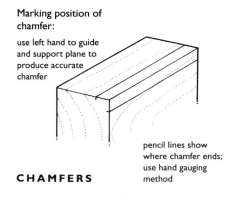

pencil lines show where chamfer ends; use hand gauging method

CHAMFERS

ROUNDS

position of first chamfer

second intermediate bevel

third bevel produces flat areas so small they can easily be sanded

SPLAYS AND BEVELS

A splay or bevel is a sloping surface. If it runs from one side of a piece of wood to the other it is best to mark a pencil line on both faces of the wood rather than trying to work to an indefinite top corner. Work in the same way as a chamfer.

ROUNDS

Rounds are formed by creating a series of chamfers. Mark on the pencil gauge lines as you would for a single chamfer but also show on both ends of the wood a round of the correct radius. Work this chamfer as normal but do not go all the way down to the pencil gauge lines – just work to the circumference of the round. When you have reached this line you will have created two ridges, so bevel these two corners as though trying to create intermediate splays (see illustration page 70), working each one at a time. Do not try to alter the position of the plane in an effort to 'corkscrew' the edge into a round.

Next plane off the new ridges created by the secondary bevels and continue the process, until eventually the ridges left by planing are so small that you can merely sandpaper the edge round. It sounds complicated – but takes seconds!

HOW TO CREATE
DECORATIVE MOLDINGS ON EDGES

WITH A COMBINATION PLANE

Combination planes produce a variety of moldings on straight edges, though it can be difficult to stop and start a molding part-way along an edge. With some methods of frame construction, this can make both the marking out and cutting of the joint quite a complicated process. Also, a combination plane cannot easily work moldings around corners or produce curved work.

SCRATCH STOCK

Usually home-made, a scratch stock consists quite simply of two pieces of wood made into an 'L'-shape, which sandwich a blade in place. The 'L'-shape produces a natural fence to guide the blade and keep it a uniform distance from the edge of the wood being worked.

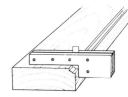

Cutting moldings

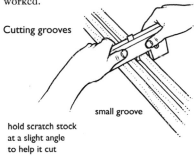

Cutting grooves

small groove

hold scratch stock at a slight angle to help it cut

> **IMPORTANT**
>
> Make sure you do not let the scratch stock wander away from the edge as you use it, or the molding or groove will be ruined.

A scratch stock cuts like a cabinet scraper, with a burr edge acting as a very fine cutter. The problem with using a scratch stock is getting it to cut without roughing up the work. You can make your own moldings for the blade on a small electric grinding wheel and as long as this burr is pushed along the wood it will cut. If it does not, adjust the angle of the stock until it does.

You can use a scratch stock along the grain for cutting small grooves, for inlays, or for preparing and cleaning up moldings. When working grooves across the grain, score the wood carefully with a knife first, actually to cut the fibers. The scratch stock then scoops out and removes the wood left between the knife lines.

SANDING MOLDINGS

If you are having difficulty in sanding a molding – perhaps you cannot get into a tight corner properly or are damaging other areas of your work – make up a small sanding block which has the reverse profile of the molding itself. Use a fine or light-weight paper which fits around the block to follow its contours. Use this to sand the molding along the grain.

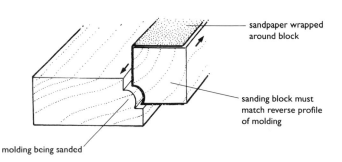

sandpaper wrapped around block

sanding block must match reverse profile of molding

molding being sanded

CUTTING AND FITTING JOINTS

Woodwork joints are mostly held together by interlocking pieces of wood, or adhesives, or both. On some occasions nails or screws may be used, either for speed of assembly or extra strength.

Sometimes, as with dowel or loose tongue joints, a separate piece of wood provides the strength of a joint. In others, such as in a dovetail joint, the strength lies in the way the wood itself is cut.

Joints have evolved into their present-day form mainly for two very specific reasons. First, a good fitting joint can be incredibly strong, enhancing the natural properties of wood as a constructional material. Secondly, if it is well proportioned, a joint can also be used as an aesthetic feature in a piece of furniture.

To make properly constructed joints you will need to practice layout, cutting and fitting.

GOOD HABITS

- Always mark the waste clearly in pencil. Number the joints.
- Use a knife to mark shoulder lines that are to be sawn or pared back to.
- Always cut on the waste side of a line, just touching it.
- Always hold the work steady and support the waste – use a bench hook if appropriate.
- Remember that joints can only be as good as the care you take in laying them out.

Whether for decorative effect or strength, always choose the right joint for the job. Screws or nails can sometimes provide additional reinforcement

MITERS

Miters are one of the simplest means of jointing two pieces of wood. This can be at any angle, but is most often at 90 degrees. Miters are commonly used on picture frames where the joint would be held in place with glue and perhaps strengthened with veneer or panel pins. They are also used on frames, plinths and beads around panels.

It is relatively easy to use a combination square to mark the position of the first halves of two miter joints on one length of wood only (see page 29), but to copy this information to the other pieces is harder. These guidelines should help.

LAYOUT

After marking the miters on one piece of wood, put any others to be mitered at the same length one at a time, back to back with the first. Next, mark on the positions of the new miters with a knife or sharp pencil. Continue these markings around the edges of the wood using the combination square. This will give an exact line to saw to.

CUTTING

Put each piece to be cut in a miter box with the knife line just to one side of the saw slot. Protect the miter box with a block and hold the wood firmly with your hand. Always adjust the wood in the box so that the kerf (see page 27) of the saw will run down the waste side of the joint. Make the knife line down the back edge of the miter bolder if this helps you produce a clean saw cut.

Let the saw do the work. Do not force it. If you do, the joint will be inaccurate and you could damage the miter box.

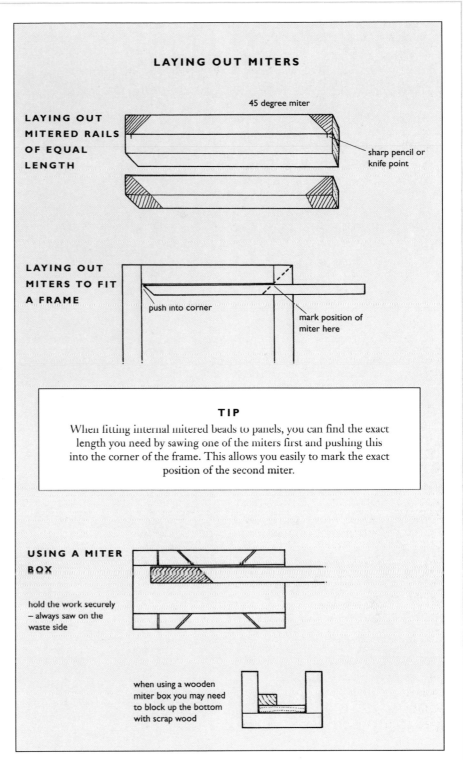

LAYING OUT MITERS

LAYING OUT MITERED RAILS OF EQUAL LENGTH

45 degree miter

sharp pencil or knife point

LAYING OUT MITERS TO FIT A FRAME

push into corner

mark position of miter here

TIP
When fitting internal mitered beads to panels, you can find the exact length you need by sawing one of the miters first and pushing this into the corner of the frame. This allows you easily to mark the exact position of the second miter.

USING A MITER BOX

hold the work securely – always saw on the waste side

when using a wooden miter box you may need to block up the bottom with scrap wood

TIP
Cut the longest lengths to be mitered first – then, if you make a mistake, you can cut these down and make them into shorter ones.

GLUING

When gluing up a mitered frame, use miter clamps or frame clamps. The joints of large, mitered constructions such as plinths on furniture can be strengthened with blocks which are glued, or screwed and glued into place. These are known as glue blocks.

TIP
Assemble small frames in a vise if you don't have a miter or frame clamp. Glue each joint in turn using pins to keep them in place.

DOWEL JOINTS

Dowel joints are simple in concept. A dowel is a cylindrical wooden peg with the grain running along it. This is fastened into two corresponding holes in separate pieces of wood. Once they are held in place with glue, dowels look no different from a traditional mortise and tenon joint, but they are nowhere near as strong. The biggest challenge is making the two holes match each other exactly.

HOW TO MAKE A DOWEL JOINT

To join two pieces of wood by use of dowels to make a T-shape:

METHOD ONE

1 Using a marking gauge, mark a center line on the end of piece A from the face side.

2 Mark a matching center line on piece B, again from the face side. Light pencil marks will help you see where to start and stop this center line.

3 Using a marking gauge, mark measured gauge lines on the end of piece A where the center of the dowels should be. To ensure that these correspond on piece B, transfer these markings with a knife and square to make a cross, while both pieces are firmly clamped together in a vise.

METHOD TWO

Lay out piece A as in Method One, but drill the holes and then insert center pins into them. Offer up piece B; the center pins will leave tiny pinpoints on piece B in the correct position, ready for drilling.

METHOD THREE

If you need to lay out and cut several dowel joints you can use a dowel jig. One disadvantage is that it may take some time to set up.

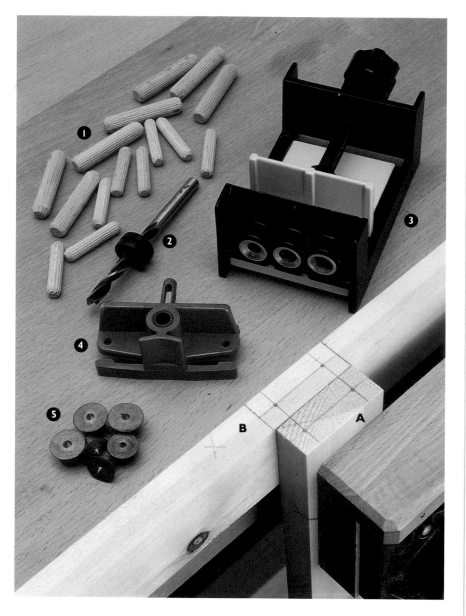

CUTTING A DOWEL JOINT

1 Use a metal pointer to make a clear mark at the center of the crosses on both pieces of wood.

2 Drill both A and B making sure that the holes are exactly at 90 degrees to the layout surfaces. A drill stand may help.

3 Fit dowels first to piece A and glue them in place. Ribbed dowels allow glue to escape so that the dowel does not trap the glue as it is pushed home.

4 While the glue is still wet, offer up piece B to piece A and clamp tightly.

Dowel joints are simple to make and an easy way of fastening two pieces of wood together. Here, pieces A and B are shown marked out ready for drilling (see methods 1 and 2)

1 Dowels
2 Drill bit and drill stop
3 Dowel jig
4 Simple dowel jig for jointing chipboard panels
5 Center bits

BUTT JOINTS AND EDGE JOINTING

BUTT JOINTS

A butt joint on a corner couldn't be simpler. It is important to mark the shoulders with a knife (see page 62) and to saw exactly to this line. The saw cut must be accurate, although a light skim with a smoothing plane will produce a cleaner surface for the glue to bond to. Follow the instructions on page 70 to ensure that the grain does not tear out at the back.

Where extra strength is needed it is wise to use glue blocks. These can be glued in place or screwed and glued: either way, they strengthen the joint. In furniture making, this sort of butt joint is most often used for the back joints of a plinth assembly.

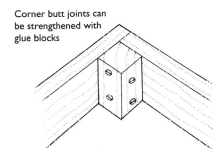

Corner butt joints can be strengthened with glue blocks

DOVETAIL NAILING

Butt joints can be strengthened by dovetail nailing, where nails are driven into the joint at alternating angles. This is a simple technique that gives a butt joint extra strength. Insert the first nail at the center of the joint, square-on, in the usual way, to stop the butt joint moving around. Then dovetail nail on either side of the first nail.

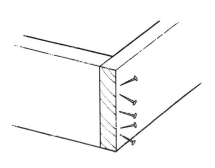

EDGE JOINTING

marks showing how boards join

alternate rings

The illustration on page 69 shows how to plane one edge perfectly square. Edge jointing two boards together relies on preparing two edges in this way, and then fitting them together.

A good edge joint (sometimes known as a rub joint) should not rely on tongues or dowels to keep it together. When complete, the joint should hardly be visible and you certainly should not see any trace of a glue line.

Select the pieces of wood to be joined for their attractive figure, and if you can, fit the boards together with the growth rings arranged alternately for stability: by doing this, if there is a slight amount of movement, both boards will cup in different directions, making the boards much easier to flatten again with hand planes. Mark the boards with a pencil line to show where they go and prepare the edges with a try plane. Next, put one of the pieces in the vise and offer the other one up to it. Have some light behind the joint to help you see whether there are any gaps between the two boards. Adjust the piece held in the vise as necessary by taking off just one or two shavings with the try plane. This is not difficult but perfecting the technique takes some practice. While they are still in the vise, make sure that the two boards sit perfectly on top of each other. Check with a straight edge.

Select the boards to be joined for figure and mark them clearly in pencil

Check that they join exactly using natural or artificial light behind the joint. If there is a tiny gap take off one more shaving

Use a straight edge to check the joined boards lie straight and do not lean

EDGE JOINTING – A SECOND METHOD

This method is suitable for short lengths of wood only, and it relies on the convex nature of the plane blade. Put both pieces of wood together in a vise and plane them both at the same time. Remove them from the vise and turn one of them over: they should fit together, to produce a very quick butt joint.

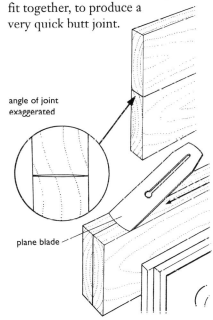

angle of joint exaggerated

plane blade

TIP

At first you may not feel confident enough to rely solely on an edge butt joint and you may prefer to strengthen it. Here are some ways you could try.

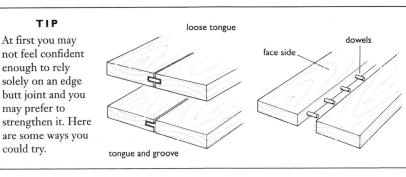

loose tongue

tongue and groove

face side

dowels

THE MORTISE AND TENON JOINT

The mortise and tenon joint is perhaps 'the' most basic of woodwork joints – the school woodwork joint that everyone struggled with. It utilizes the strength of wood by interlocking one piece of wood with another.

LAYING OUT A SINGLE MORTISE AND TENON JOINT

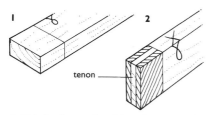

1 Mark four shoulder lines with a knife on the piece that will have the tenon. Work from the face side and face edge (see page 62).

2 Use a mortise gauge, set up to the width of your mortise chisel to mark the position of the tenon. This should be roughly central and about a third of the total thickness of the wood. Show the waste clearly.

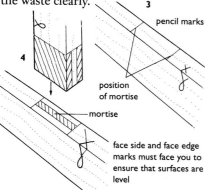

pencil marks

position of mortise

mortise

face side and face edge marks must face you to ensure that surfaces are level

3 Mark the length of the mortise on the second piece with light pencil lines. You can use the width of the tenon as a template to help establish the length of the mortise.

4 Go over the pencil lines with a knife to show clearly the position of the mortise. Use the mortise gauge at the same setting as the tenon to mark on the width of the mortise. Work from the face sides on both pieces, so that the tenon corresponds to the mortise. Again mark the waste.

CUTTING OUT

Once the joint has been laid out you can start cutting. The quality of the finished joint depends very much on how good you are at using a saw and chisel. Follow the gauge lines, correcting yourself as soon as possible if you wander from the line. Do not rush, work carefully and do not allow the saw to bind. A little paraffin wax will help the saw blade to cut smoothly. Keep checking as you saw that you do not go past the marking gauge lines.

HOW TO CUT THE TENON

1 Put the piece of wood with the tenon marked on it into a vise at an angle of around 45 degrees. Standing sideways to the bench front, use a tenon saw to cut down to the shoulder line facing you. Cut down both cheeks of the tenon whilst in this position.

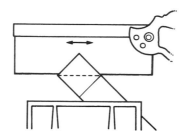

2 Turn the piece of wood around and (again at around 45 degrees in the vise) cut both cheeks of the tenon from the other edge.

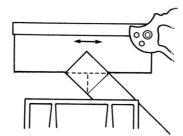

3 Now saw fully down to the shoulder line. This time, hold the wood upright in the vise and continue sawing down the saw cuts you have already made, being careful not to go past the shoulder line, especially at the back.

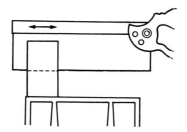

4 Next, use a saw board or bench hook to cut the shoulders and to remove the waste pieces which will fall off as you saw. A 'vee' will help you start sawing (see page 26).

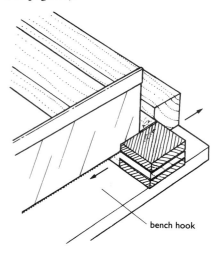

bench hook

5 Clean up the corners of shoulders carefully with a chisel if necessary.

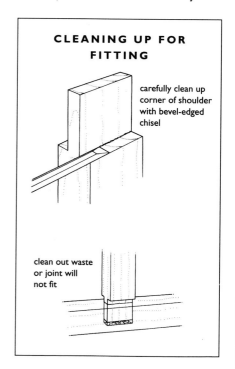

CLEANING UP FOR FITTING

carefully clean up corner of shoulder with bevel-edged chisel

clean out waste or joint will not fit

Mortise and tenon joints can take many forms. Here are a few:

1 Loose wedge mortise and tenon
2 Stopped mortise and tenon
3 Molded frame mortise and tenon
4 Through mortise and tenon

HOW TO CUT THE MORTISE

1 Hold the work on the bench securely with an F or C-clamp, protecting it with an offcut of wood. Protect the bench too, with another offcut used as a cutting board.

2 (A–D) Use a mortise chisel and mallet to cut the mortise, as shown right.

3 Make sure that the bottom of the mortise is clean and flat, checking with a depth gauge if necessary. The mortise should be around ¹⁄₁₆in (2mm) deeper than the length of the tenon. This will avoid a 'glue trap' which may prevent the joint from being pushed together during assembly.

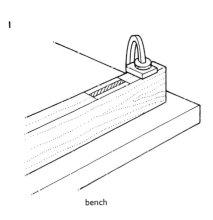

bench

2A
start in center with chisel upright

B
work toward you cleaning out the waste

C
turn chisel around and work away from you again cleaning out the waste

D
with the mortise hole clear of waste make a final clean cut down each shoulder line

Be careful as the chisel may creep back slightly as you cut.

3 check the mortise is of uniform depth

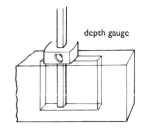

depth gauge

FITTING

There is usually a little cleaning up to do after sawing (see left, page 76), the biggest problems being the shoulders of the tenon and the bottom of the mortise. If both halves of the joint are accurately cut, they should fit snugly together. If they do not, check to find out why and adjust them accordingly.

HALF-LAP JOINT

A half-lap joint is so-called because in theory you remove half the thickness of each piece of wood, so that each part fits snugly into the other. There are three variations – the cross lap, the T-half-lap and the corner lap.

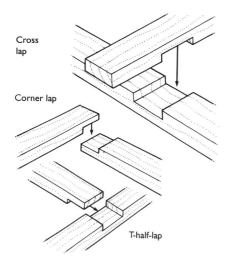

Cross lap

Corner lap

T-half-lap

HOW TO LAY OUT A CROSS LAP JOINT

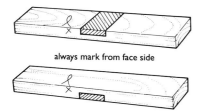

always mark from face side

Lay out the lap joint on each of the two pieces of wood to be joined, putting the knife-lines on only one face and two edges. Note that one piece will have knifed markings on its face side while the other will have knife lines on the side opposite the face side. Both pieces will be laid out on their edges.

To establish the width of the joint, use one half of the joint as the template to guarantee that both will fit each other exactly.

Next, use a marking gauge set to about half the thickness of the wood. It does not need to be exact, as long as both pieces match each other later. This is guaranteed by working from the face sides. You must use only one setting on the gauge to ensure both halves fit.

HOW TO CUT A LAP JOINT

Cut each piece in turn, preferably holding it against a bench hook. Saw down both sets of knife-lines, working on the waste side. Work to the gauged shoulder lines but do not go past them.

Now hold the timber in a vise. Use a bevel-edged chisel (bevel down) to remove part of the waste. After working from one side, turn the wood around and work from the other side.

Finish off by cleaning up to the marking gauge line, by horizontal paring with the chisel, this time, bevel up (see page 42).

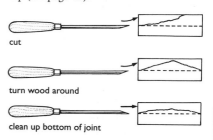

cut

turn wood around

clean up bottom of joint

BRIDLE JOINT

The bridle joint has two common forms, the corner bridle joint and the 'T' bridle joint. They are marked out in a similar way to mortise and tenon joints.

The corner bridle joint has a straight-forward tenon on one half, which is cut using the same technique as that shown on page 76. The other half of the joint (known as the mortise) is best cut out as follows.

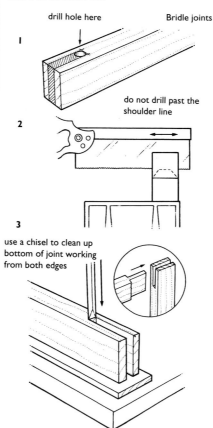

drill hole here   Bridle joints

1

do not drill past the shoulder line

2

3

use a chisel to clean up bottom of joint working from both edges

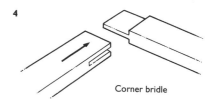

4

Corner bridle

1 After laying out the position of the mortise, drill a hole near the shoulder line the same width as, or a little less than, the mortise itself.
2 Saw the cheeks as you would saw a tenon, eventually meeting up with the hole.
3 Clean up the bottom of the bridle joint with a bevel-edged chisel, working from both edges so that you don't tear out the wood on the back edge.
4 Check that the joint fits and adjust accordingly.

HOW TO CUT A 'T' BRIDLE JOINT

Cut the mortise as for a corner bridle joint. Cut the tenon as for a lap joint – but instead of working to half the thickness with a marking gauge, you will have to work to a third of the thickness and use a mortise gauge.

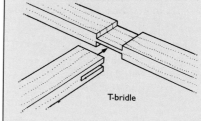

T-bridle

DADO JOINT

Dado joints are often used on traditional bookcase shelving. There are two variations on the normal through dado – the stepped dado and the sliding dovetail. Housing joints are either cut as through joints, or 'stopped' so that the joint is not seen on the front edge of a carcase.

HOW TO LAY OUT A DADO JOINT

On a through dado the shelf-part of the joint is laid out like a simple butt joint. Measure the length of the shelf and use a knife and square to mark two sets of knife lines around all four surfaces. Mark the waste. Ensure that after cutting, all ends are square and of the same length.

On the component that will become the bookcase side, mark the top position of the joint using a sharp pencil and try square, lining in with a knife. Continue these lines in pencil only, to roughly half-way down the front and back edges. You can then use the shelf as a template to establish the exact width of the joint, marking this position too.

From the face side, mark the depth (about one third to one half the thickness) of the dado joint on the back and front edges with a marking gauge, using the pencil lines as a guide to how far to go. Now go over the pencil lines with a knife. Label the waste.

STEPPED DADO JOINT

On a stepped dado, after cutting the shelf to length, lightly plane the ends and use a cutting gauge to lay out the shoulders of the joint. The thickness of the joint can be scribed on the end with a marking gauge.

TYPES OF DADO JOINT

Through dado

Stopped dado

Stepped dado

Sliding dovetail

A stopped, barefaced dado joint – a neat, strong joint for shelving

---

HOW TO CUT A DADO JOINT

Use a tenon saw to cut the sides of the trench and remove the center of the joint by using a hand-held router plane. If the joint is stopped, cut a mortise at one end of the trench first to saw into. When using the saw to cut the trench, clamp on a piece of wood just to one side of the knife-line to act as a guide. Always saw on the waste side.

TIP

If you prefer you could use an electric router held against a stop that is clamped in place, but work carefully and slowly so that you do not slip.

MORE COMPLEX JOINTS

THE DOVETAIL JOINT

The dovetail joint is one of the strongest and most decorative joints of all. There are many sorts of dovetail joint, but the two most common types are those used on drawers – the through dovetail (at the back) and the lapped or half-blind dovetail (at the front).

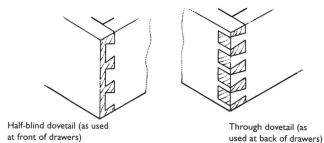

Half-blind dovetail (as used at front of drawers)

Through dovetail (as used at back of drawers)

Knife lines on joints should be crisp, accurate and deep enough to cut the fibers of the wood

LAYING OUT THE THROUGH DOVETAIL JOINT

The through dovetail should be quite easy to lay out as long as you follow a logical procedure.

Let us use a drawer as an example. The width of this drawer is 4in (100mm) and there are to be three dovetails. The width of the pins is to be ¼in (6mm) – which is the width of the chisel you will use to remove them later. The width of the side pins is to be ⁵⁄₁₆in (8mm). (Usually the number of dovetails is a matter of personal choice.)

Marking the dovetails

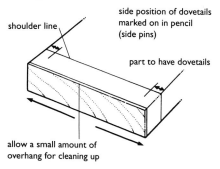

shoulder line

side position of dovetails marked on in pencil (side pins)

part to have dovetails

allow a small amount of overhang for cleaning up

Fact: if there are three dovetails, then the pins in between them (excluding the side pins) must always number two (see opposite).

You will need a ¼in (6mm) bevel-edged chisel, two pairs of dividers, a pencil and a knife.

Always keep the face sides of all pieces making up the drawer pointing inwards. Mark shoulder lines on both pieces to be joined, allowing around ⅓₂in (0.5–1mm) overhang for cleaning up (see also page 89). On the piece that has the dovetails, lay out as follows:

1 Set up one of the pairs of dividers to the width of the ¼in (6mm) bevel-edged chisel that will be used to cut out the pins, plus ⅓₂in (0.5mm) (to allow for clearance). From the left-hand ⁵⁄₁₆in

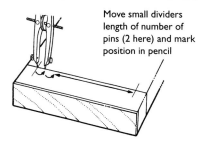

Move small dividers length of number of pins (2 here) and mark position in pencil

(8mm) pencil line marking the position of the end pin, use the dividers to count two ¼in (6mm) 'spaces'. Mark this position with the point of a sharp pencil.

Fact: the space that is now left between this pencil point and the right-hand side pin is exactly the same as the combined length of the three dovetails you need. If you divide this space into three, it will equal the width of one of the dovetails.

2 Take the second pair of dividers and set them to what you estimate a third of this space to be, then adjust the dividers slightly until they are actually set at the correct width: this should only take seconds.

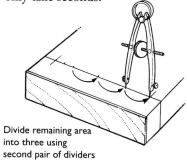

Divide remaining area into three using second pair of dividers

IMPORTANT

If you are laying out more than one joint, do not lay them out fully one at a time, but complete each step on them all and only then move on to the next stage.

3 Next mark the position of the first dovetail, starting from the left-hand side pin, using the second pair of dividers. Then locate a pin (with the first pair of dividers), then a dovetail, then a pin, and finally a third dovetail. You will finish exactly at the position of the right-hand side pin. Mark the points clearly with the end of a knife as you go and you will easily see where the two pins and three dovetails should be.

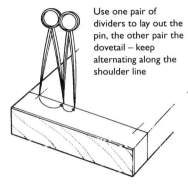

Use one pair of dividers to lay out the pin, the other pair the dovetail – keep alternating along the shoulder line

4 After this, hold the wood upright in a vise and use a dovetail gauge and knife to lay out the dovetails, both on the face of the wood and across the end too. Label the waste clearly.

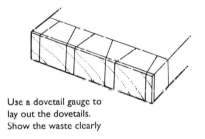

Use a dovetail gauge to lay out the dovetails. Show the waste clearly

HOW TO CUT A THROUGH DOVETAIL

So far, you have laid out the dovetails for only one half of a dovetail joint. Cut these out before laying out the pins on the second piece of wood.

Hold the wood in a vise and saw each dovetail on the waste side down to the shoulder. Keep checking at the back that you have not gone too far.

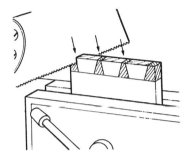

Saw one set of angles and then alter your position to cut the second set

Remove the ⅜in (8mm) end pins from each side with a tenon saw. On the bench chop out the two central pins with the ¼in (6mm) chisel, paring back cleanly to the line from one face only. Use a chopping board to stop the wood spelching out at the back.

Once you have cut out the dovetails for this half of the joint you can use it as an exact template for the other half. It is crucial that you remember to number all joints clearly.

HOW TO LAY OUT THE SECOND PIECE

Lay a flat backup piece – say a square piece of ½in (12mm) thick plywood – on the bench. Hold the piece to be laid out in a vise with the face side facing away from you. Let it protrude from the vise so that it is the same height as the backup piece. Place the other half of the joint, with the dovetails already cut, face side down on top of the piece in the vise, so that it rests both on this piece and on the backup piece. Now use a knife to mark the corresponding pins on the piece of wood in the vise. Push your left hand down on the wood to stop it moving about as you lay out the joint.

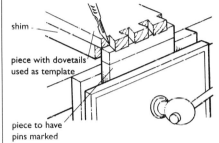

Marking the pins

push down and line up both halves of the joint

shim

piece with dovetails used as template

piece to have pins marked

Leave a tiny gap at the shoulder of the joint between the two pieces, so that you can just see light through it as you look down. This will allow for 'creep' later, when cutting out the joint. When you take the top piece off you will see the exact outline of the joint. Follow these knifed lines down to the shoulder line with a sharp pencil to help you saw accurately. Remember to label the waste.

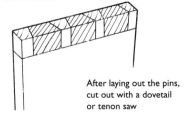

After laying out the pins, cut out with a dovetail or tenon saw

HOW TO CUT OUT THE SECOND PIECE

Saw down the pencil lines on the waste side to the shoulder, holding the work-piece in a vise. Remove the waste carefully with a coping saw, leaving around ¹⁄₁₆in (2mm) to the shoulder. Clean this up by vertical paring back to the shoulder with a bevel-edged chisel.

QUICK METHOD FOR LAYING OUT THROUGH DOVETAILS

When laying out dovetail joints it is essential that the pins and tails are properly spaced and that their sizes are uniform. The above method guarantees this and is especially suitable for deep drawers, boxes and chests. There is an alternative, quick, method:

After laying out the positions of the side pins as normal, simply divide the space left into the number of dovetails required (use a rule at a slight angle across the face to measure off the correct spaces if necessary) and mark these positions on the shoulder line

using a sharp pencil. Next, on either side of these pencil lines, measure half the distance of the bevel-edged chisel you are using, and mark the pins. Do not forget to add a little to the measurement to stop the chisel binding as you cut the pin. Use a dovetail gauge to continue these lines around the end and face as for the method above.

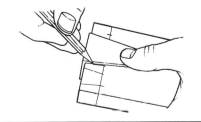

THE HALF-BLIND DOVETAIL

Cut the wood to be joined to length and then lay out the tails as you would a through dovetail joint (it is not necessary to allow any overhang), but ensure that the ends are perfectly square, as they are to be used as a template.

When laying out the pins, work in the vise as before, again using a backup piece, but this time, use your knife to mark all the way around the dovetails – i.e. along the length of the dovetails as well as across their width.

After labeling the waste, saw down the layout lines on the waste side at an angle of around 45 degrees, using a bevel-edged chisel to chop out the rest of the joint.

GOOD ADVICE

- Always fit joints (or tap them apart) with a hammer, not a mallet, and use a protective block. Do not try to pull joints apart by hand, especially dovetails and mortise and tenons as they easily damage.

- Always work exactly to the knifed shoulder lines and expect the chisel to creep slightly when cutting out. Double check that you have removed all the waste from the bottoms of joints (especially in tight corners) as it is never a wise policy to rely on twisting on a clamp to try to force a joint into place.

- When putting dovetails together, test whether they will work by pushing them only part-way in – never more than half-way.

- Always support the work properly and always cut on the waste side.

- When gluing up very tight dovetail joints you can use dovetail blocks to help push the joints into place (see page 87).

When cleaning up a joint do not cut further back than the shoulder line or the two parts will not fit together correctly

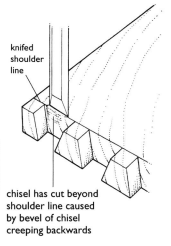

knifed shoulder line

chisel has cut beyond shoulder line caused by bevel of chisel creeping backwards

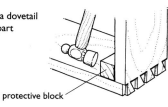

Taking a dovetail joint apart

protective block

TECHNICAL TALK

LOOSE TONGUE Thin strip of wood/plywood inserted into a joint to strengthen it.

VENEER PINS Used to tack veneers and hold very small moldings in place.

CENTRE POINTS Small cylindrical metal inserts with a point at one end. Used to mark out the positions of dowels

FLUTED DOWEL Dowel that is ribbed along its length, allowing glue to escape.

PARAFFIN WAX White-colored wax used for candle-making. Ideal for lubricating wooden components (e.g. drawers); and waxing saw blades and plane soles.

CUTTING BOARD (chopping board) Scrap piece of wood used to protect the bench top while chopping out joints. It must be smooth, flat and undamaged to protect the workpiece.

DADO A long, narrow groove running across the grain of a piece of wood.

DOVETAILS AND PINS Two halves of a dovetail joint. Dovetails are wedge-shaped extensions, usually wider than the pins, which are the slender extensions that fit into the gap (eye or socket) between the dovetails.

DOVETAIL GAUGE Tool used to guarantee a uniform angle for dovetails.

CREEP The small distance a chisel wanders from a knife line due to its bevelled cutting edge.

DOVETAIL BLOCK Clamping block with finger-like extensions which push dovetails into place, allowing pins to fit in-between.

ASSEMBLING AND GLUING UP

It is at the gluing up stage that theory is put into instant practice.
Rushing around and wiping glue off with damp rags is all part of the job –
but there's no need to panic.

When you are ready to assemble a piece of furniture it is a good idea to do a trial glue-up (dry assembly) first. This will allow you to ensure that everything goes together as it should and that you have the right tools, such as clamps, at hand.

HOW TO DO A DRY ASSEMBLY

As the purpose of the trial run is to make sure things fit, before you start you should check that all joints are properly cleaned out and that they have been cut exactly to the layout lines. Then put everything together, following the numbers on your joints. Next identify any offending joint or area that needs more attention, take everything apart again and adjust it. If you are still not absolutely sure that the joints will go together perfectly, do a second dry assembly.

The more experienced you become, the more this trial glue-up will be of use in making sure that you have everything at hand for gluing rather than for checking the joints. But for a beginner, this stage can make all the difference in the world to the look of the finished piece.

When gluing up it is always a good idea to have someone with you who can help to hold and steady long bar clamps and clamping blocks, as they can very easily be the cause of dents and bruises on wood.

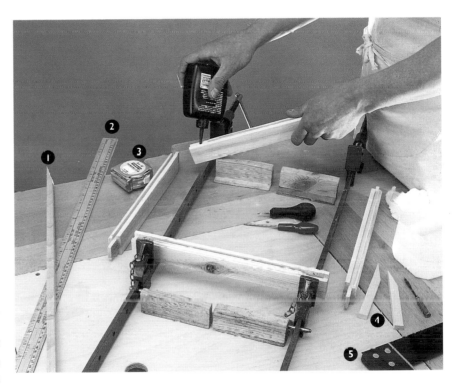

CLAMPING BLOCKS

Your clamping blocks should all be of the same thickness, so check that they fit in the clamps. Make sure they are all clean and undamaged. They should not be made of a harder material than the wood you are gluing up – for example, do not use oak blocks to glue up softwood furniture.

As well as clamps and clamping blocks, you also need a few pointed scrapers (homemade wooden ones are handy), some rags and a tub of water, for wiping off the glue.

Gluing up a simple frame: bar clamps and clamping blocks are shown in position. Always have a pot of water and a cloth handy for wiping down

1 Squaring rod
2 Steel rules
3 Tape measure
4 Steel and wooden pointers for removing excess glue
5 Try square

GLUING A SIMPLE FRAME

Assembling and gluing a simple frame construction, such as a door with traditional mortise and tenon joints, is quite straight-forward. Bookcases and other pieces of furniture with more complicated constructions can be more troublesome (see page 85).

For a simple frame, first prepare the bar clamps and blocks and lay them out at roughly the right distance apart from each other on a floor or flat surface. Put the (as yet unglued) frame components in their relevant positions so that there is no confusion over where each one goes.

One of the easiest adhesives to use is PVA (see page 87), which is white or yellow in color. When dry, it produces a very strong bond on bare wood, if it is clean and free from oil and grease.

Apply PVA adhesive to one half of the joint only, or in accordance with manufacturer's instructions. With mortise and tenon joints it is best to squeeze it into the mortise. Do not be too liberal: if you use too much glue at this stage you will despair later, when glue is running everywhere or when

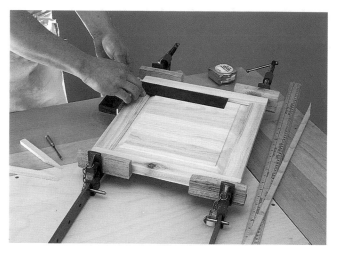

After gluing a simple frame together, check that it is square and flat (see below) and adjust if necessary. Leave to dry

you cannot put a joint together because of trapped glue.

Make sure that all surfaces of the joint are well covered by using a pointed stick to spread the glue around evenly. You have about 15 to 20 minutes to apply the glue and assemble the frame, so with a simple frame there is no need to rush.

After applying the adhesive, assemble the frame and put it in the clamps, which are ready and waiting. Move the

clamps a little if necessary so that they are in exactly the right position, and insert the clamping blocks. Gently tighten each clamp until it starts to bite. You will find that some glue oozes out at this stage: before clamping up too tightly, wipe this off. Don't forget to check underneath. Now clamp up more tightly, checking for square (see below) and adjusting if necessary. Next, wipe off the rest of the glue. Now all you need to do is wait.

CHECKING FOR SQUARE

During gluing, but before the frame has dried, you must guarantee that it is square and flat. To check this you can use some of these simple techniques.

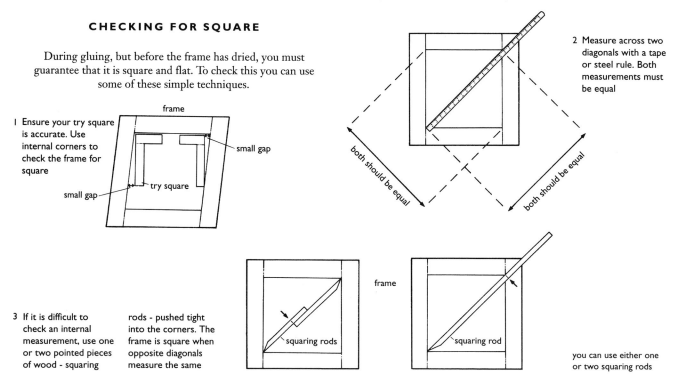

1 Ensure your try square is accurate. Use internal corners to check the frame for square

frame

small gap

small gap

try square

2 Measure across two diagonals with a tape or steel rule. Both measurements must be equal

both should be equal

both should be equal

3 If it is difficult to check an internal measurement, use one or two pointed pieces of wood - squaring

rods - pushed tight into the corners. The frame is square when opposite diagonals measure the same

squaring rods

frame

squaring rod

you can use either one or two squaring rods

GLUING UP
MORE COMPLEX PROJECTS

Being organized when gluing up difficult constructions makes all the difference.

Assembling a simple frame is relatively easy because there are only four right-angles to check. Also, you have plenty of time before the adhesive becomes unworkable. This may not be so with more complex projects.

You will need to handle all the clamps and other tools you use during gluing quickly, but carefully. Take extra care not to damage anything as you work.

As an example, assume that you are gluing up the bookcase shown in the projects section of this book, on page 112. In this particular case, the best procedure for gluing is as follows.

Prepare your clamps (see page 84). Lay one bookcase side on the floor and apply glue to the dado joints and mortises. Use a small stick to spread the glue around the joints. Repeat for the other bookcase side.

Next, insert the shelves and rails into one of the sides – let gravity do the work for you. Now comes the tricky part: preferably with the help of someone else, quickly lift and turn the

second bookcase side over and locate the relevant joints, tapping them into place with the palm of your hand. On some projects you may have several joints to locate, so you must work quickly to stop the glue running out of the joints.

When you have located all the joints, turn the bookcase on its back and sit it on the prepared bar clamps. Gently tighten them with clamping blocks in place. Put more clamps on the front of the bookcase and gently tighten them. Wipe off any excess glue, and then fully tighten all clamps. Check for square.

With bookcases or wide components you may find that the center of the sides bellies outwards as the clamps are tightened. This is caused by trapped glue or air and is cured by the use of

cauls — curved clamping blocks designed to increase the pressure at the center of the bookcase side. You can cut these yourself.

Chairs and other awkward shapes are usually best supported with frame clamps or web clamps, or even a loop of string tightened with a stick. Drafting tape will help keep small components in place as they dry (see page 87).

Finally, do not be afraid to hit a joint (protected by a block) quite firmly with a hammer to knock it into place. However, before you use the hammer, make sure that the only reason for the joint not going home is because it is a good tight fit. If not, you are likely to hear a stomach-churning splitting sound . . .

Gluing up more complex projects can occasionally become quite a hectic experience, but as long as you are prepared for all eventualities by careful organization and especially by performing a dry assembly first of all, then things should run smoothly and work according to plan.

Bar clamps holding a complex carcase together during a dry assembly. Make sure that all clamps are directly in line with the shelves, base and top rails as shown

HOW TO GLUE EDGE JOINTED BOARDS

1 If you use wood that has been planed on two faces, it is easy to select boards for matching figure. Prepare the edges to be jointed for gluing (see page 75). Mark these faces clearly with a pencil.

2 Put bar clamps on the floor, with their centers 18–24in (450–600mm) apart. Long boards may need several clamps.

3 Lay the boards on the clamps and dry clamp them to ensure the joints are good and will go together.

4 Undo the clamps and apply PVA adhesive to one edge only of each joint. Leave the adhesive for about 3–4 minutes to change color from white to pale grey, but do not let it dry out.

5 Clamp the boards together again and wipe off any excess glue. There may be a slight amount of 'bellying up' as you clamp up. This can be rectified by adding more clamps in-between the others, but on top of the boards, rather than below. Make sure the boards lie flat on the bottom clamps. Some woods, such as oak, may discolor because of a chemical reaction between the wood and the glue. If this is a problem, use spacers between the clamps and the wood, making sure they are of equal thickness to ensure the wood remains flat.

If the boards are still not flat, or if the problem is extreme, the probable fault is that the edges have not been planed square. If this is the case, the only remedy is to go back to the workbench and practice your planing.

After gluing, leave the boards to dry, then remove the panel from the clamps. Clean up the faces with a smoothing plane (see page 89). If there has been a slight amount of distortion during gluing up, you can rectify this by lightly working over the surface first with a jack or fore plane.

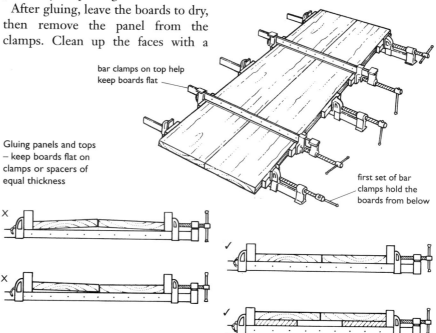

bar clamps on top help keep boards flat

first set of bar clamps hold the boards from below

Gluing panels and tops – keep boards flat on clamps or spacers of equal thickness

---

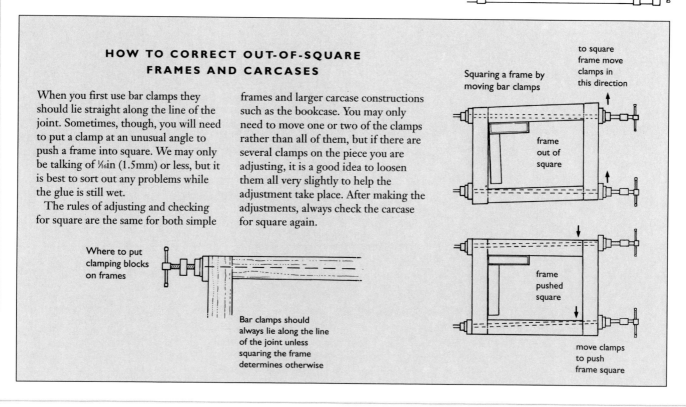

HOW TO CORRECT OUT-OF-SQUARE FRAMES AND CARCASES

When you first use bar clamps they should lie straight along the line of the joint. Sometimes, though, you will need to put a clamp at an unusual angle to push a frame into square. We may only be talking of $\frac{1}{16}$in (1.5mm) or less, but it is best to sort out any problems while the glue is still wet.

The rules of adjusting and checking for square are the same for both simple frames and larger carcase constructions such as the bookcase. You may only need to move one or two of the clamps rather than all of them, but if there are several clamps on the piece you are adjusting, it is a good idea to loosen them all very slightly to help the adjustment take place. After making the adjustments, always check the carcase for square again.

Squaring a frame by moving bar clamps

to square frame move clamps in this direction

frame out of square

frame pushed square

move clamps to push frame square

Where to put clamping blocks on frames

Bar clamps should always lie along the line of the joint unless squaring the frame determines otherwise

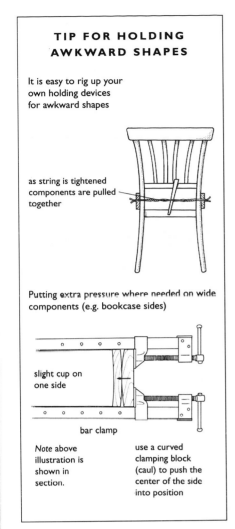

TIP FOR HOLDING AWKWARD SHAPES

It is easy to rig up your own holding devices for awkward shapes

as string is tightened components are pulled together

Putting extra pressure where needed on wide components (e.g. bookcase sides)

slight cup on one side

bar clamp

Note above illustration is shown in section.

use a curved clamping block (caul) to push the center of the side into position

TYPES OF ADHESIVE

As the chemistry of adhesives is complex, the descriptions here offer a basic guide and so are not clouded in technical jargon. For general woodwork there are four basic types: scotch/hide glue, suitable for internal woodwork only; PVA (emulsion) adhesive; two-part adhesive, and impact/contact adhesive. There are also 'hot-melt' glues used in glue guns – these are suitable for veneer work.

PVA (EMULSION) ADHESIVE

PVA is available in formulations suitable for either external or internal work. It is strong and very easy to use. Allow 15–20 minutes of working time during assembly. Beware, though – if the glue is allowed to dry on bare wood, white marks become highly visible on subsequent finishing.

HOW TO GLUE DOVETAIL JOINTS

Dovetail joints may be glued together using clamps like other joints, or they can be left unclamped if the joint is fully together and tight. If you do clamp them, it is a good idea to make up a set of dovetail clamping blocks, which will deliver increased force where it is needed. Apply PVA adhesive to the half of the joint with the pins, spreading it on all internal faces. Assemble the work and use bar clamps and clamping blocks to clamp up from the center dovetail. Clamp alternate dovetails one at a time, working toward the edges. Once the joint is pushed home (a hammer and block may help stubborn joints), clamp up again tightly along the line of the center of the joint.

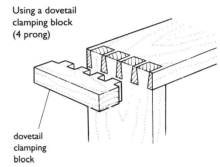

Using a dovetail clamping block (4 prong)

dovetail clamping block

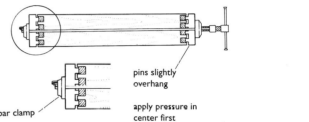

bar clamp

pins slightly overhang

apply pressure in center first

SCOTCH/HIDE GLUE

A traditional glue made from animal hide and bones. Also known as animal glue. Suitable for use on internal parts only, and usually bought in the form of pearls. Soak these pearls first in water, before heating in a glue pot. Scotch glue is easy to sand off the surface of wood and generally does not mark the work. Any glue left in the pot can simply be reheated, making it immediately ready for use again. The disadvantage of animal glue is that it is not particularly strong (certainly not as strong as PVA) and as it cools and gels very quickly it can make the gluing up of large projects difficult.

A major bonus for furniture restorers working on older pieces that have been glued with Scotch glue, is that the gentle heat from a hair dryer or a little warm water in a syringe will easily soften the glue again. Thus the joints can be taken apart for repair and reglued. Decorative inlays and bandings are usually glued in place with animal glue.

TWO-PART ADHESIVE

This term covers dozens of adhesives, including urea formaldehyde, resorcinol and epoxy resins. The adhesive comes in two parts, a resin and a hardener, and the mixing of these in specific ratios produces a reaction, giving each adhesive its own properties. Two-part adhesives are often used where waterproof or extremely strong glue bonds are required, some being especially suited to very heavy duty work.

IMPACT/CONTACT ADHESIVE

The most suitable type of adhesive for bonding plastic laminate or for small areas of veneer work. Thinly spread the glue on both faces and leave a short while for it to become tacky. The glue bond is either formed the second the two faces meet or as soon as pressure is applied, depending on the particular adhesive. Whatever happens, do not put veneer in the wrong place if working with impact adhesive, or you will regret it.

CLEANING UP

No matter how carefully you have made your joints, after gluing there are bound to be some parts of a construction that are not quite flat or level. Cleaning up corrects these slight errors.

How do you know when to clean up each part – before or after gluing? The simple rule of thumb is to clean up and sand all internal faces, such as the inside of a drawer, prior to gluing. This allows you to deal with tight corners. You can clean up and sand external surfaces later.

HOW TO CLEAN UP A SIMPLE FRAME

To clean up door stiles (end grain), work to an accurately marked knife line. Hold the work in a vise and plane inward toward the rest of the door. This will stop the fibers of the wood tearing out (see page 70).

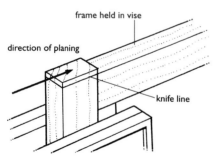

frame held in vise

direction of planing

knife line

To clean up a bookcase shelf or rail that stands proud, work inward, which will give the plane more control and prevent damaging the bookcase side.

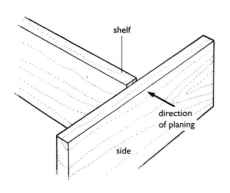

shelf

direction of planing

side

Sometimes you may have no choice but to clean up by planing in a direction that is not the most suitable, especially if the grain is tearing up badly. If so, take extra care, ensure the plane is sharp and remove only one shaving at a time.

Cleaning up the underside of a plinth carefully using a smoothing plane

HOW TO CLEAN UP A TOP EDGE

To clean up constructions that are jointed at right angles, slide the plane around at 45 degrees to create a slicing action. This will prevent damage to the pieces of wood you are not planing and will produce a better cut. When making up drawers, if you can, select the wood for the sides so you plane from the front to the back of the drawer. This will stop you damaging the top edge of the front by planing across it.

Take care with cleaning up. If you try to speed up the process, especially by planing across the grain on frames, the damage will be seen when you come to polish.

After planing, check the surface again and remove any torn grain with a cabinet scraper only if essential (see page 35). Now you are ready to sand.

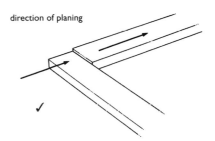

direction of planing

✓

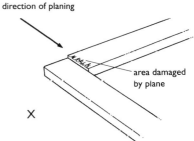

direction of planing

area damaged by plane

✗

position of plane as it moves around top edge

top two edges not level

work around a corner by slicing the plane as the direction of the grain at the corner changes: use one complete movement

HOW TO CLEAN UP A DOVETAIL

Hold the dovetail joint securely in a vise. If there are any gaps in the joint repair them before cleaning up by filling them with a mix of very fine wood dust and glue. Use a sharp, finely set, smoothing plane to work the surface. Always plane toward the main body of the drawer or box. If the wood is particularly hard or difficult, you can use the plane in a circular motion to slice the wood, which will stop any grain from tearing out.

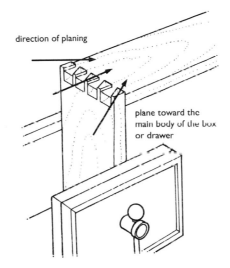

direction of planing

plane toward the main body of the box or drawer

TIP

If PVA adhesive is allowed to dry on bare wood, a pale or white marking will appear during subsequent finishing. If it is possible, sand the wood and apply two coats of finish/sealer (see page 97) before gluing so that you can easily wipe off the glue with a damp cloth. The faint grey markings left on the surface will instantly disappear on application of a further coat of finish.

GOOD ADVICE

Make sure that you always check the plane blade for sharpness and re-sharpen before starting to clean up. When working with tough woods such as oak it may be necessary to re-hone the plane blade at quite regular intervals to maintain a keen edge.

HOW TO CLEAN UP EDGE JOINTED BOARDS

When edge jointed boards are removed from the clamps, there will always be some cleaning up to do. There may well be a slight ridge where the boards meet at the joint or a small amount of cupping may take place if the wood adjusts to new surroundings while you are working on the rest of the project. These new surroundings might even constitute changes in the weather, especially during periods of

extreme heat or damp (see page 11). These can be removed with a smoothing plane. If there is any torn grain produced during planing, remove this using a cabinet scraper.

When you have checked the panel for being flat using a straight edge (see page 67), trim to size.

Finally, prepare the edges ready to accept any moldings and then sand ready for finishing.

SANDING

Sanding wood takes time. But without proper sanding it is impossible to achieve a professional finish.

Sanding removes the marks on the surface of wood caused by hand planing or scraping. The process is to use a coarse grit of abrasive paper to flatten the surface of the wood, and then to work through several grades of paper, getting finer each time, to remove any scratches left by the previous, coarser paper. Eventually, the scratches produced by sanding become so small that the eye cannot see them. It is only at this point that the wood is ready for finishing.

You will achieve more control when sanding by hand if you use a block (wrap a thin cloth around it if you wish) rather than your fingers. Never use an orbital sander on work that is to be finished as it will leave tiny circular scratches on the surface of the wood, totally ruining it.

HOW TO SAND

Garnet paper is particularly suited to top quality work as it is kind to the wood. The grade of paper you start with depends on whether the wood is already quite smooth from the plane or not. For most furniture, start with 80 or 100 grit garnet paper, and then work through the grades – 150, say, followed by 220, and finishing with 320. On softwoods you can finish with 180 grade instead of 320, and on open-grained hardwoods, such as oak, you can finish with 220 grade. There are more details on which grade to use on page 93.

If the surface is already quite smooth, do not start with a grade as coarse as 80 – instead use 120 or even 150 grade. It is important to let each grade do its fair share of the work. Beginners often have a tendency to work through the intermediate grades too quickly. A very fine paper will easily remove the marks left by a paper that is just a little more rough than itself, but it will never be able to remove the scratches left by a coarse one.

Left Machine cutter marks show up as faint bruises under strong light. During finishing these stand out if not removed with a bench plane

Right Torn grain caused where the fibers of the wood have been pulled out. Don't fill but remove using a cabinet scraper (see page 35)

TIP
Never plane work that has already been sanded – the blade will soon become blunt if you try.

TIP
If you see fine dust gathering in small pockets on the surface as you sand, this is an indication of damage or of a slight hollow. Check to see exactly why the dust is collecting where it is, rather than just simply wiping it off.

Always sand along the grain, never allowing the sanding block to sweep the surface in an arc and never let the paper clog up, as this will cause damage to the wood.

Preparation of the surface is complete when all the defects have been removed, the wood is flat and it feels silky smooth to the touch. I cannot overstate the importance of sanding, especially on top quality work.

TIP
Areas that are difficult to get to, such as the insides of small boxes, are best sanded and part-finished before assembly. Ensure, though, that you do not get any finish on the joint as this will stop the glue bonding to the wood.

WOOD FILLERS

Wood fillers are used to repair defects by filling holes and cracks. Do not confuse these with grainfillers, which are used to fill the pores of the wood prior to finishing (see page 97). Never use a filler on torn grain. Although there are several types of filler available, you can repair some defects without using them at all.

TIP

Always select a filler which matches as closely as possible the final color of the wood as most will not satisfactorily stain later. After using a filler you can use earth pigments to paint 'grain' or an artificial knot back on to the wood before polishing. This will help to conceal the defect.

USING FILLERS

TYPE OF FILLER	HOW TO USE	DEFECT REPAIRED
Beamontage: home-made blend of rosin (tree resin) and pure beeswax. Mix in equal parts (melt the rosin first) with a little pure turpentine and make into a stick	Soften a piece between fingers. Push into hole with screwdriver tip. Leave to dry. Clean off with a chisel, plane or by sanding. Harder than wax filler sticks. Color with a little oil stain	For filling very small holes
Wax sticks: a proprietary blend of waxes	Use in the same way as beaumontage	For filling small holes and hair-line cracks
Shellac sticks: sold in a range of colors. They are quite brittle and break easily	Melt a little of the stick into the hole with the end of a soldering iron. Use a chisel tip to press in and sand smooth	For repairing small holes or cracks before applying a high gloss finish e.g. French polish
Powder based fillers: a mix of wood dust and powder made into a paste. Available in several colors or make by mixing PVA adhesive and fine wood dust	Select a suitable color and fill the hole. Plane surface flat; then sand off. They become much darker when stained and finished	For use of small holes on lower quality work or where the defect will not be clearly visible

---

DEFECTS THAT DO NOT REQUIRE A WOOD FILLER

CRACKS AND SPLITS IN NEW WOOD

Cracks and splits in new wood are easily repaired and you can be sure the joint will be as strong as the wood itself. Put the wood in a vise and gently lean against it, opening up the crack. Squeeze PVA adhesive into the crack. Turn the wood around, leaning on it again to open it up from the other side. Squeeze glue into this side too. Next, use a vise, C-clamp or bar clamps to push the crack tightly together. Wipe off any excess glue and leave it to dry. Finally, clean up with hand planes and sand.

CRACKS AND SPLITS IN OLD WOOD

If the wood is old and stable it is better to fill the split with a sliver of wood that will match the figure and appearance of the existing wood, rather than use a filler. Any small gaps still left can be filled with colored wax filler sticks, or beaumontage, and can even be painted out later if necessary.

DENTS

If a dent has just been created on unfinished wood, lay a damp cloth on the dent, and using the tip of an electric iron, simply steam it out. As wood is made up of long, relatively hollow cells, steam puffs the crushed cells back out. It takes around 15–20 minutes for the dent to disappear – if the last little bit does not steam out, either plane the surface smooth again or level the small hole with a filler. Finally, sand the wood smooth.

Steaming out a dent (bare wood only). Wet area around dent with clean water. Press iron on damp cloth to steam out the defect. Repeat steaming for up to 20 minutes until dent is lifted out. Leave to dry. Resand, or replane and resand ready for finishing

dent

iron

damp cloth

TYPES OF ABRASIVE PAPER

There are many abrasive papers suitable for sanding wood. The table opposite gives some idea of comparative grit sizes but remember that as some abrasives are softer they will blunt more quickly. In general woodwork the latter is a disadvantage, but there are times when it is actually an asset. Flour paper, for example, loses its cutting edge very easily (producing a much finer abrasive than the chart would seem to indicate), and is therefore excellent for wood finishing, being able to denib (rub down) polish without damaging the surface. (See page 98.)

FLINT PAPER

Tan or pale-brown in color, this is usually less expensive than most other abrasive papers. It blunts quickly during sanding.

GARNET PAPER

Made from industrial garnet crystals, which have the advantage of breaking while in use, constantly producing a new supply of cutting edges. Garnet paper is most suitable for hand sanding fine cabinet work.

ALUMINUM OXIDE PAPER

Generally mid-brown to grey in color, aluminum oxide papers are much tougher than garnet papers. This makes them ideal for hand sanding very dense hardwoods and for use with sanding machines.

SELF LUBRICATING SILICON CARBIDE PAPER

A pale blue/grey paper, the most useful grades of which are 320 and 400 grit used in finishing. These are especially useful for denibbing finish as they cut extremely well and have a slightly lubricated feel.

WET 'N DRY PAPER

A dark-grey silicon carbide paper, more often used in metalwork. Grades 600 to 1200 are sometimes used to denib tough varnishes and lacquers or for fine sanding.

SANDING BLOCKS

Sanding blocks are readily available in wood, cork or rubber or you can just as easily make your own from an offcut. The important thing to remember is that the block should be a little softer than the wood you are sanding, or it will damage the surface. Before using a block make sure that its face is flat and smooth.

If you use a cork block or a very soft rubber one, take care to ensure that it does not round over the edges you are sanding instead of keeping them square and crisp.

One final word of warning, when sanding edges, look out for those long, needle-sharp splinters. It really does hurt if one happens to pierce its way through the paper into your hand.

When sanding, make sure that you do not accidentally round over edges as this will prevent them from looking clean and crisp

COMPARATIVE GRADES OF ABRASIVE PAPERS

FLINT PAPER Blunts easily	GARNET PAPER Suitable for hand sanding	ALUMINIUM OXIDE PAPER Suitable for wood- working machinery	SILICON CARBIDE PAPER Use finer grades for denibbing; coarser grades for metal work
			600*
		400	400*
	9/0 or 320	320	320*
	8/0 or 280	280	280
00 or flour*	7/0 or 240	240	240
0	6/0 or 220	220	220
	5/0 or 180	180	180
1	4/0 or 150	150	150
1½	3/0 or 120	120	120
F2	2/0 or 100	100	100
	0 or 80	80	80

* Suitable for denibbing
Note very coarse grades of paper have been omitted from the chart

1 Garnet paper
2 Aluminum oxide paper
3 Flint paper
4 Wet 'n dry paper

FINISHING

Wood finishing seems an incredibly complex subject, but it
can be surprisingly simple too. It is easy to achieve a professional looking finish
as long as you know what to do, and in what order to do it.

One of the challenges in finishing is knowing which products are compatible – i.e. which stain goes with which top coat. Get it wrong and the result can be disastrous, and you may even have to start again. The information below gives black-and-white guidelines, but of course, there are always exceptions to any rules, so if you have even the slightest doubt, make sure that you consult your supplier.

WHAT STAINS ARE BASED ON

Most stains and finishes suitable for home woodwork use will dilute in one of these three bases:

- Water
- Methyl alcohol (methylated spirit – denatured alcohol)
- Oil (derived from petroleum – hydrocarbons)

In addition, there are also natural finishing oils, such as tung oil and linseed oil. Other products, such as cellulose lacquer, are much more specialized, and are not included here.

Using a polishing mop to apply thin coats of French polish

HOW TO DECIDE WHAT TO USE

If you choose a stain with a similar base to the finish you want to use, the two will try to blend together, and the most probable result will be a patchy finish. At the very least, the polish will become contaminated with the color of the stain. Select a stain with a different base to that of the polish; it will seal the stain in and protect the wood.

STAINS

Stains are used to color woods. This could be to enhance the grain, change the color of the wood (perhaps to match another, more expensive, wood), or to make new furniture blend into existing surroundings. Stains do not protect the wood. Some modern 'colored finishes' – which are actually varnishes – are unfortunately and confusingly called wood stains.

FINISHES

Finishes seal the wood, protecting the surface, stopping it becoming soiled or finger-marked. Finishes reveal and enhance the figure and beauty of wood. Some finishes, such as French polish can, in practised hands, produce an incredibly high decorative shine. Generally, you need to select a finish that you feel will offer the best combination of protection and sheen.

HOW TO FINISH

Houses are built on foundations that are level and properly
constructed; similarly, in wood finishing, the wood must be flat (with any defects repaired
and holes filled) and sanded smooth before staining and finishing begins.

WHAT TO USE

Oil finishes and wax polishes are easy to work with (two coats of sanding sealer before waxing will protect against finger-marking); French polish can be used to produce a decorative sheen/high gloss or if more protection to the surface is required, use a varnish.

THE PROCESS

The basic rules of finishing are:

Finish → denib → clean

1 Finish – apply a thin, even coat of finish, allowing it to dry properly in-between coats.

2 Denib – rub down the surface with fine abrasives to flatten it.

3 Clean – remove any dust from the surface, using a clean cloth or a 'tack cloth' (a special sticky cloth used to collect dust). On bare wood you can use a rag damped with methyl alcohol to clean the wood but you must allow this to dry before starting to finish.

The finishing process is essentially the same even for products like French polish. For example, a polisher's rubber (a pad made of cotton wadding with an outer cotton layer) is designed to put on very thin layers of finish.

TIP

To remove tiny particles of dust from a finished surface, gently touch it with the corner of a piece of abrasive paper. The dust will simply stick to the paper and lift it off.

Materials for basic finishing:

1 Soft mutton cloth for wax polishing
2 Paste wax
3 Polishing mop suspended in a jar of French polish
4 Dust removing cloth
5 Ultra fine 0000 grade steel wool
6 Polishing mop
7 Sanding block and fine abrasive paper

a

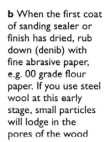

d

b

e

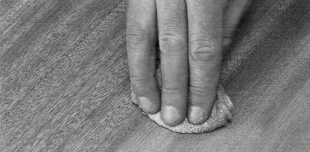

c

a Try not to lead on to the surface as this will cause the finish to run down the edge. Instead, let the mop or brush glide off at the edges

b When the first coat of sanding sealer or finish has dried, rub down (denib) with fine abrasive paper, e.g. 00 grade flour paper. If you use steel wool at this early stage, small particles will lodge in the pores of the wood

c Always remove the dust after denibbing each coat of finish

d After the first two or three applications of finish (don't forget to rub down and clean off the surface between each one), you can move on to a finer abrasive. Here, 0000 grade steel wool is being used to denib the surface

e Finally, after cleaning the surface, apply wax polish with a soft cloth and leave for a few minutes to soak in. Buff off for a professional looking natural sheen

HOW-TO GUIDES

There are many finishing products, which offer different degrees of protection and shine. Each product has its own method of application, and the purpose of the following guides is to help you to produce a professional finish without first having to become a master finisher. Although the process is always to stain first and then finish, it is wise to select the finish first and then choose a stain, if you need one, that is compatible. You should always practice on scrap wood first, never on the real thing.

OIL FINISHES

OIL FINISHES – PENETRATING OILS Do not confuse oil finishes with petroleum-based, manufactured products. Finishes such as tung oil, can occur quite naturally, although they may also contain chemicals to speed up the finishing process. Oil finishes are very easy to apply.

Oil finishes seal and protect the wood by first soaking into the surface and then hardening. Apply a reasonably liberal first coat and leave it to soak in for 10–15 minutes or more, before wiping off the excess. Leave the rest of the oil to soak into the wood completely before buffing – this is crucial. The drying time for some proprietry brands of oil finish is 4–8 hours, but you will need to leave pure tung oil as long as 24 hours between coats. If you use raw linseed oil as a finish, thin it with pure turpentine (2 parts oil to 1 part turpentine) before use.

After the first coat of oil has dried, apply further coats much more sparingly. Always leave enough drying time. You may like to rub the surface down between coats with 0000 steel wool to help flatten the oil and pull out the sheen. Always rub along the grain. Apply a minimum of three or four coats to produce a satin sheen. Maintain the surface by re-oiling at regular yearly intervals or when required. For specific product information, read individual manufacturers' guidelines.

Note if you have a problem with the oil remaining sticky on the surface, you are probably applying it too thickly, or you are not taking off the excess oil correctly.

WAX POLISHES (PASTE WAXES)

Wax polishes, like oil finishes, are easy to use. Simple as they are, though, there are some pitfalls. There are two basic types of paste wax polish, those that go straight on to bare wood and those intended for previously sealed or finished surfaces – it is wise to choose the correct one.

WAXING BARE WOOD

Apply the wax polish to the wood sparingly with a soft cloth. It feeds and seals the surface as it soaks in. Leave it for anything from 3–30 minutes after application, depending on the wax, until the surface is ready for buffing with a soft cloth.

It takes many coats of wax polish to build up a proper sheen, and the wax will require a great deal of buffing, which can be hard work. One problem is if you apply the coats too thickly, as the wax will build-up in corners and look unsightly.

WAXING SEALED AND FINISHED WOOD

To speed up the waxing process, you can apply a sanding sealer to the wood first. Two to three coats of sanding sealer (or even white French polish, used as a sealer) will achieve a quick shine which will not become finger-marked (see Sanding Sealer). To speed up the process on pine furniture, you could apply the wax along the grain with 0000 steel wool, instead of a soft cloth, after the final coat of sealer. You must, however, use a soft cloth to buff the wax back off again.

You can make your own wax polish by simply mixing beeswax with pure turpentine, perhaps stiffening the mix a little with carnauba wax.

Note liquid waxes are used for intricate surfaces such as old beams or doors. Do not use spray waxes on bare or sealed wood. The above instructions are for paste wax polishes only.

1 White/clear paste wax
2 Colored paste wax
3 Shellac sanding sealer
4 Penetrating oil (oil finish)
5 Colored oil-based grain filler
6 Natural oil-based grain filler

SANDING SEALER

Sanding sealer acts as a foundation for other finishes, which are applied on top of them. It is not a finish in its own right, but is extremely useful as a base for both wax polish and French polish.

First make sure the wood is smooth, clear of dust and does not have any old finishes left on it. Apply each coat of sanding sealer with either a cotton cloth or a brush, ensuring that the sealer uniformly covers the surface of the wood. Leave it to dry and then denib along the grain (see page 98) with a fine abrasive paper, such as flour paper or 400 grit silicon carbide paper. Clean off the fine dust produced and apply another coat of sealer. Always denib between coats and keep the surface free of dust. Two or three coats of sanding sealer will generally be sufficient before proceeding to further finishing. Denib the last coat of sealer with 0000 grade ultra-fine steel wool instead of the flour paper if you prefer.

To create a simple finish using sanding sealer and wax polish:

1 Sand the wood and clean off dust.
2 Apply first coat of sanding sealer; denib; clean.
3 Apply second coat of sanding sealer; denib; clean.
4 Apply third coat of sanding sealer; denib; clean.
5 Apply paste wax polish, buffing off with a soft cloth.

DIFFERENT COLORS

French polishes, as well as being clear, are also available in different colors. At times these are useful for adding tone to wood without having to mix up special polishes of your own (see page 101).

Note the secret to French polishing successfully with a rubber is to apply many very thin coats, working all of the surface to push the polish deep into the pores of the wood. Because of this, French polishing using a rubber is a lengthy and complicated process (see page 155 for books that will help).

FRENCH POLISH

There is an easy and effective way to apply French polish using a brush or polisher's mop. (See note below on using a polisher's rubber.)

If applying French polish with a brush or mop, the secret is to thin the polish slightly in methyl alcohol and use it as you would sanding sealer. However, you can apply many more coats than with the sanding sealer, building up the shine as you go. If you use this method, finish by denibbing the final coat with 0000 steel wool and applying a paste wax polish to protect the wood. The final result will be a very natural looking, easily achieved, high shine on the wood, but not an extremely glossy 'piano finish'.

GRAINFILLERS

Grainfillers (which should not be confused with wood fillers, used to fill holes – see page 91), body up the surface of wood by filling the pores before finishing. They are used as a foundation for French polish or where a higher shine is required. Grainfillers either consist of superfine plaster of Paris mixed with water, or are available as factory-produced oil-based products. In both cases you apply them across the grain with a coarse rag to push the filler deep into the pores of the wood. Before the filler has dried completely, wipe off any excess filler with a new piece of rag. Grainfillers are not necessary for simple, basic finishing but are useful in more advanced finishing.

Your choice of finish should be determined by the amount of shine and durability required

Left French polish
Right Oil finish

HOW-TO GUIDES

VARNISHES AND LACQUERS

Varnishes are effectively clear paints. They offer very good protection to the surface of the wood without obscuring its figure.

Water-based varnishes, which are often described as acrylic varnishes, tend to look milky, and leave the surface with a slightly cloudy appearance after drying. However, the advantage of water-based varnishes is that they offer good protection, are very quick-drying, non-flammable and, importantly, are safe to use.

Manufacturers can increase or reduce the amount of solid content in a varnish, which determines whether the varnish produces a matte, satin or a gloss finish. Varnishes differ in this respect from products such as French polish, where it is the number of coats applied to the surface of the wood that dictates the depth of shine. You can buy colored varnishes, although be careful when applying these by brush or you may see brush strokes.

Varnishes offer much more protection than oil finishes, wax polishes or French polish, but they can make the wood look artificial.

Lacquers are similar to varnishes, producing a very decorative, glossy surface coating on internal woodwork. Modern spray lacquers have been developed to produce a very hard-wearing, quick-drying gloss finish, which is often an attempt to imitate the glossy 'piano finish' of French polish.

DENIBBING

Denibbing is the name given to the process of rubbing down between coats of finish. After a coat of finish has dried, little bumps are left on the surface. Denibbing removes these bumps.

It is important during denibbing to rub along the grain and not across it or in an arc. In the early stages of finishing you can denib quite heavily, but do not rub so hard that you break through the finish you have already applied. Be especially careful if you have stained the wood first. You must cover the whole surface uniformly and the process is only complete when the nibs have been removed and the finish looks perfectly flat. Check this by inspecting the surface of the wood closely, looking for any areas which are more shiny. Denibbing is of great importance on any surface that will become a feature, such as a table top.

In the very early stages of denibbing use either 00 grade flour paper or 400 grit self lubricating silicon carbide paper rather than 0000 steel wool, webbed pads or powder abrasives. Papers will not break up leaving unwanted foreign bodies in the pores of the wood, and if used with a sanding block will also keep the first layers of polish much flatter.

You can change to 0000 ultra-fine steel wool or fine webbed pads after the first few coats of finish have sealed the surface of the wood.

French polishes:
1 Transparent
2 White
3 Button
4 Orange
5 Garnet

Varnish:
6 Polyurethane
7 Acrylic (solvent-free) water-based

Shellac flakes:
8 Blonde dewaxed (for transparent polish)
9 Button
10 Garnet

WHAT TO USE WHEN APPLYING FINISHES

WHAT TO USE	FINISH	COMMENTS
Ultra fine '0000' grade steel wool	First coat of wax	Steel wool may damage the surface unless applied along the grain only or use steel wool first and then apply wax with a soft cloth
White cotton/soft cloth	Oil finishes, wax polish, sanding sealer	Wax should always be buffed off with a very soft cloth such as a mutton cloth
Polishing mop	Sanding sealer, French polish, modified French polishes	Allows controlled thin coats of finish to be applied if used properly
Polisher's rubber	French polish	With practice, allows polish to be pushed into the pores of the wood, building up a high shine
Brush	Varnish, French polish, sanding sealer	Brush strokes may remain visible as finish dries
Varnish brush	Varnish and some lacquers	A fine brush to apply thin coats of varnish
Specialist spray equipment	Lacquers	Industrial use: for repetitive finishing

MATERIALS FOR DENIBBING

Some of the products listed below are not suitable for basic finishing. Follow each How-to Guide for best results.

00 GRADE FLOUR PAPER Use for initial denibbing. As the abrasive particles blunt easily, rub on a scrap piece of wood first to produce a fine abrasive paper before starting to denib.

320 AND 400 GRADE SELF LUBRICATING SILICON CARBIDE ('LUBRISIL') PAPER Very fine cutting paper suitable for slightly harder finishes such as varnish, as well as sanding sealers and French polish.

600 TO 1200 WET 'N' DRY PAPER Use for denibbing very hard polishes and lacquers. On some lacquers, wet 'n' dry paper may need to be lubricated with a finishing oil to help it cut.

0000 (PRONOUNCED 'FOUR NOUGHT') WIRE WOOL Made up into a soft wire pad to rub down polished surfaces. It can sometimes give light coloured woods a pale grey tone.

WEBBED PADS Manufactured pads such as Scotchbrite, produced in specific grades as an alternative to steel wool. They have the advantage of not clogging during use. Ideal on curved surfaces including carvings and turnings.

PUMICE POWDER, French chalk and rottenstone powder abrasives, used in either a cotton pouch called a 'pounce bag' (which is simply rubbed along the polished surface) or put between the wadding and cotton outer of a French polisher's rubber to help keep the polish flatter (this process is known as grinding). Recommended for more advanced finishing only.

BURNISHING CREAM/PASTE Not specifically used for denibbing. They contain an extremely fine abrasive and are used to cut back potentially shiny surfaces such as cellulose lacquer and French polish, to produce a very high gloss. The surface being burnished must have a full polished finish.

SIMPLE TIPS FOR LOOKING AFTER FINISHED FURNITURE

SCRATCH MARKS If the scratch has broken through the finished surface and bare wood is visible, apply a small amount of wood stain to the scratch to blend it in. Deeper scratches may need filling with colored wax. Very fine scratches can be removed from surfaces that are not high gloss by lightly rubbing along the grain (covering the whole surface) with 0000 steel wool and rewaxing.

WATER MARKS Often visible as a white bloom mark on the surface of the finish. If the water has penetrated the wood the surface may feel rough and refinishing may be necessary. If not, rub along the grain with 0000 steel wool and rewax. A little thinned raw linseed oil on the steel wool may help.

RING MARKS For light markings only, abrade the surface gently and rewax (see water marks above).

CLEANING FURNITURE (prior to rewaxing) Older furniture may need rejuvenating to bring back its color and sheen. Either use a proprietary brand of cleaner or make your own by mixing together one part raw linseed oil, one part white vinegar, one part methyl alcohol and one part turpentine. Test on a small area first.

TECHNICAL TALK

FRENCH POLISH Made by dissolving shellac (derived from the deposits of the laciffer lacca beetle) in methyl alcohol. Available in many colors: transparent, white (clear), button (yellow), orange (orange) and garnet (brown).

CARNAUBA WAX A hard natural wax, also known as Brazilian wax.

POLISHING MOP Finishing tool used to apply much thinner coats than a paint brush. Not generally used to apply varnish.

LINT-FREE COTTON CLOTH Has no synthetic content.

HOW-TO GUIDES

HOW TO STAIN WOOD

As with finishes, there are also special types of stain, but they are not generally available in small quantities and for the sake of simplicity have not been included here.

There are three main bases for wood stains:

- Water
- Alcohol or spirit – denatured methyl alcohol
- Oil

To lighten the color of any stain, find out what it contains and dilute it in its own base chemical.

BASIC WOOD STAINS

ALCOHOL-BASED STAINS

Available in powder form for preparing your own colors, or as a ready-made liquid stain. If you choose stains from the same manufacturer's range, each color should be intermixable with the rest so you can produce a wide variety of new colors and shades. Alcohol stains are best applied by cloth. Do not confuse methyl alcohol with naphtha (white spirit), which is used in conjunction with oil-based stains.

TIP

If you use powder stains to color French polish (see page 101), add them to a little methyl alcohol first, before introducing to the polish. This will help to distribute the stain evenly throughout the polish.

OIL-BASED STAINS

You can easily identify an oil-based stain because it will dilute in paint thinner or naphtha. Oil-based stains are the easiest wood stains to use; most wood stains in hardware stores are oil-based. These stains give you a little more time to work. Apply by cloth or by brush. If you do use a brush, remove the excess stain before it has dried with a lint-free cotton cloth. Oil-based stains are not usually light-fast and are therefore not suitable for antique restoration work.

Make sure that before you apply any finish to the wood, the oil stain is quite dry. This takes around 24 hours. If after this time the stain is still sticky, you have applied too much or not wiped it off correctly.

WATER-BASED STAINS

Water-based stains will sit beneath most finishes. They are usually light-fast, producing deep, subtle colors. They are harder to work with than oil stains, but have the advantage of safety, since they are not flammable.

Water-based stains are available in powder form as well as liquids and you can easily mix up your own colors. They are best applied by brush. Wipe off the excess stain after a few seconds with a clean lint-free cotton cloth.

The one major disadvantage of water stains is that, as with all water based products, they raise the grain of the wood. To overcome this you must raise the grain first, before staining.

SAFETY

Some of the chemicals contained in wood stains may be poisonous. Always take suitable precautions.

REMEMBER

If the chemical stain you use is water-based, you must raise the grain of the wood first, as with all water-based stains.

Staining: always keep a live/wet edge as you work across a surface

a Apply stain along the grain with lint free cotton cloth

b Or, apply a thicker coat of stain to the surface with a brush. Do not let the stain dry out. Wipe off along the grain with a lint free cotton cloth

TRADITIONAL STAINS AND CHEMICAL STAINS

Some stains are produced from natural products and others react with the wood to create a new color. Vandyke crystals are one of the most popular traditional stains. These are actually made from walnut shells, and produce a subtle brown color, which is especially useful on oak. Dilute the flakes in hot water to create your desired shade and then strain off any residue. Use Vandyke crystals as you would a water-based stain.

CHEMICAL STAINS

These are chemicals that genuinely stain wood rather than just dyeing it, by reacting with chemicals in the wood itself, which in turn creates a deep color or shade. There are dozens of old recipes for chemical stains and certain woods such as oak, mahogany and walnut readily lend themselves to this type of staining. The depth of color produced depends on the strength and size of the reaction and because of this, components such as rails may require color toning to make them match the rest of the piece.

One bonus with chemical stains is that if you select two woods, one that reacts with the chemical stain and one that does not, you can create good contrasts between the two, which is especially useful on inlaid work.

TRADITIONAL CHEMICAL STAINS

BICHROMATE OF POTASH (POTASSIUM DICHROMATE) This is a very common chemical stain, which produces a traditional brown shade on European oak and a grey/brown shade on American oak. Brazilian mahogany darkens to a lovely, rich shade of red-brown. Pine develops a patchy yellow tan which can look a little like antique pine. On American walnut the bichromate makes the dark purple much browner, so that it almost resembles European walnut.

Bichromate of potash reacts with many woods, although most pale-coloured woods are either not affected or darken only very slightly. Some light-coloured woods may take on a very unattractive green/yellow tone.

TOOLS FOR STAINING

BRUSH Brushing puts stains on more thickly than a cloth and generally produces a darker shade on wood. Water-based stains are best applied by brush, along the grain, evenly covering the surface. Leave the stain to soak in for a few seconds, and wipe the excess off again along the grain, with a lint-free cotton cloth.

COTTON CLOTH Ensure the cloth is lint-free – i.e. with no synthetic content, or the stain will slide around on the surface rather than being pushed into the wood. Make up a small pad and dab it in the stain, taking off any excess on the back of a sheet of old sandpaper. Apply the stain to the wood, always along the grain from one end to the other and always working from a live edge – i.e., the edge where you left off in order to recharge the pad with stain. Using this method allows you to work carefully from one edge of a wide board to the other.

If you produce patchy work, you can re-stain the work, or, in the case of water-based stains, wipe over the surface with a dampened cloth to redistribute the stain.

RAISING THE GRAIN Wood, as we know, swells as it absorbs moisture. If you apply any water-based product to a newly sanded surface, the fibers expand and the surface becomes quite rough again. The liquid content of water-based stains and varnishes always produces this effect on wood, and it cannot be rectified after staining by sanding the surface.

To overcome this problem you must first raise the grain yourself. Sand the work smooth and then wet the wood with clean water, using a cloth. Next, leave the wood to dry. You will now be able to feel the grain as bumps and ridges on the surface. Next re-sand, using the finest grade of abrasive paper that you used to sand before (do not over-sand) – this will flatten the fibers again. Clean off any dust and then stain the wood. The grain will now not lift during staining.

COLOR TONING

If you have stained the wood first to color it, and have then started finishing, it is unwise to try to alter the color any more with wood stains, as they will not penetrate the wood but sit on top of the finish. The finishing process is always stain first, finish second. But there are times when you may need to darken an odd rail or a panel that you have started to finish. To blend this in with the rest of the piece you will need to color tone.

HOW TO COLOR TONE

Color the finish, first using a compatible wood stain. For example, polyurethane varnish (oil-based) will be colored easily by an oil-stain (i.e. those which will dilute in naphtha); whereas French finish (alcohol-based) will be colored by alcohol stains or powders (which dissolve in methyl alcohol).

Apply a lightly colored finish to the component you want to tone, instead of the clear finish being used for the rest of the work. Do not let it color any of the adjoining woodwork. Color toning is, in effect, the application of colored layers of finish, enabling one piece of wood to be blended in with the rest. Always color tone with the same type of finish you are using for the rest of the work.

When you have color toned the component sufficiently, revert to the clear finish you are using for the rest of the project. Be careful not to make the color toned area shinier than the rest by applying more finish to it than the surrounding work.

Projects

The six projects on the following pages bring together in a practical sense the information in the Tools and Techniques sections. They have been specially designed to show how to work through the stages of constructing a piece of furniture. A list of essential skills can be found at the beginning of each project. Some techniques feature as special skills, but only when they are covered in detail (with illustrations and advice) within a particular project. If the same skill is necessary for making one of the other pieces of furniture, it is simply included in the list of basic skills.

Each project has step-by-step instructions, illustrations and photographs. Working drawings show how the piece of furniture fits together, and cutting lists tell you exactly what wood you need. Always remember to number each piece of wood, and the parts of each joint, so that you can easily identify the components.

The projects progress from relatively simple to more difficult, and to build up your skills and knowledge it is best to read through them in order. To provide extra help all techniques are carefully cross-referenced. Before you start any project, read all the instructions (the information on using the working drawings and cutting lists on page 111 applies for all six projects). Try to visualize it at each stage of construction: the initial design; preparing the stock; marking and cutting out the carcase; making or fitting any embellishments and moldings; and finally, sanding, gluing up and finishing.

WORKBENCH

The workbench is probably your most important tool. Having a solid, flat work area at the right height will instantly improve the overall quality of your woodworking, helping you to gain control of the tools. This particular bench is made from hard maple or white beech, the weight of which will stop it moving around the workshop while you are planing and sanding.

HOW TO MAKE THE WORKBENCH
STEP-BY-STEP

1 PREPARING THE WOOD

Start by planing the wood straight and square (see page 66). When you have done this you can start work on the underframe.

2 MAKING THE UNDERFRAME

This is made up from simple joints, but being large, they are a little on the heavy side to cut. The underframe carcase consists of two separate end frames, each having two rails. You need to join these to the legs with mortise and tenon joints (see page 76).

The bench is designed to be taken down and reassembled as required. Therefore, the only time you will use glue in the construction (except for the top itself) is during the assembly of these end frames.

Before gluing the end frames together it is important to lay out and cut the half-lap joints for the front and back rails. There are two at the back and one at the front (three in total).

Joint the two bottom rails into the legs using dovetailed lap joints, which give more rigidity (see page 65). Then lay out the angle of the dovetail using a sliding bevel. Cut the dovetailed parts of the joint first and use these as a template for the sockets.

Use straightforward through halving joints on the top back rail (see page 78).

When you have cut out the joints and checked them for fit, sand the legs and rails and glue up the end frames, checking for square (see page 84).

3 FITTING THE TOP AND BOTTOM RAILS

When the end frames are properly dry, fit the single front rail and the two back rails using wood screws (do not use wood glue). It will help if you hold the entire frame in bar clamps, pulling the joints tight together. Drill pilot and clearance holes and insert the screws before removing the clamps (see page 51). Clean up the ends of the half-lap joints with a smoothing plane.

Dovetailed lap joints being screwed into position

SPECIAL FEATURE 1

A bench should have a good clear area all around the underside of the top, allowing you unrestricted use of C-clamps and other holding devices.

Tool well bottom and spacers in place. Note the slots which will allow for the expansion and contraction of the top

4 MAKING THE TOOL WELL

The tool well is simple to construct, being made up of just two lengths of wood, one wider than the other (see the cutting list). Use screws to fasten the wider of the two to the back rail and top edge of both end frames (the bench top forms the front of the tool well). Screw the narrower piece of wood into the first one, from the back, and at 90 degrees to it. It can also be screwed into the end frames and top back rail.

5 FITTING THE SPACERS FOR THE TOP

To allow the bench top to lie flat with the back of the tool well, you will need to screw two spacers to the top of the end frames to block up the top. I repeat, you should not glue any of these pieces in place, but remember that it is of paramount importance that the screw attachments are good.

The spacers have a series of slotted holes, allowing you to hold the bench top in place from underneath. This permits the top to move if it needs to as a result of any changes in the moisture content of the atmosphere. Chamfer the fronts of the spacers in order to remove the sharp edges.

Underside of bench showing attachment of top. Note screw at back and slot to allow for expansion and contraction

SPECIAL FEATURE 2
The open ends of the tool well are cleaned out easily with a small dustpan and brush.

WORKING DRAWINGS

FRONT ELEVATION

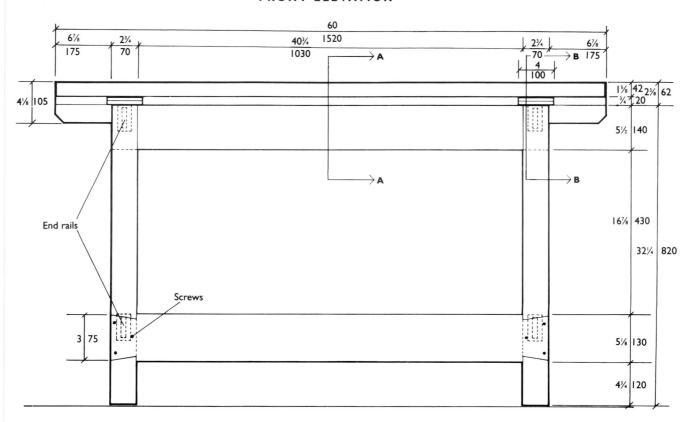

SECTION THROUGH FRONT OF BENCH B–B

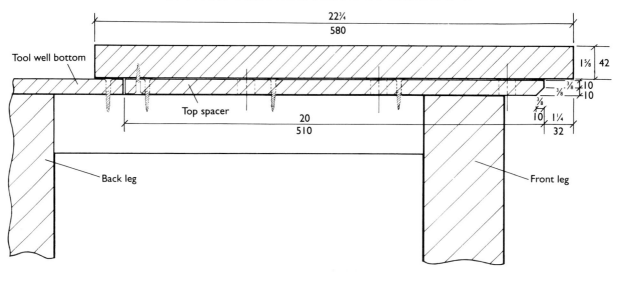

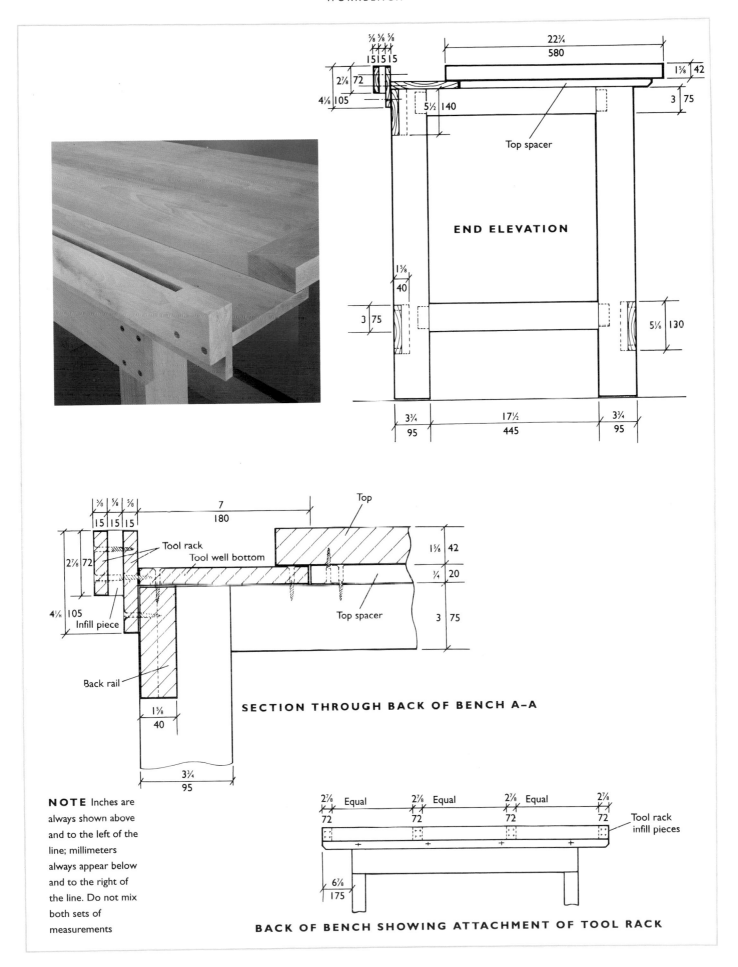

END ELEVATION

Top spacer

SECTION THROUGH BACK OF BENCH A–A

Top

Tool rack

Tool well bottom

Top spacer

Infill piece

Back rail

NOTE Inches are always shown above and to the left of the line; millimeters always appear below and to the right of the line. Do not mix both sets of measurements

Tool rack infill pieces

BACK OF BENCH SHOWING ATTACHMENT OF TOOL RACK

6 MAKING THE TOOL RACK

The tool rack at the back consists of one length of wood separated from the back of the tool well by small infill pieces of wood. These provide a gap into which the tools fit. Screw these into place. You can make the lower series of screws longer so that they fit right through the back of the tool well too. This makes for a much neater job.

7 MAKING THE BENCH TOP

The bench top is made up of four pieces of 2in (50mm) thick beech or maple, edge jointed and glued together. Follow the instructions on page 75 for preparing wide panels and tops. This particular bench has also had two end pieces fitted after the top was planed flat. However, you should fit these to a bench only if the workshop that the bench is going into has a reasonably constant temperature and humidity. If you have a garage workshop where the moisture content of the atmosphere varies widely, it is wiser to leave off the end pieces, as they may cause the top to split later.

If you do fit the end pieces, it is important to plane the ends of the top carefully so that the glue has a good surface to bond to.

Fit the bench top to the underframe through the spacers (see instruction 5, page 107).

8 FINISHING

Generally speaking there is no need to finish a workbench to the same standard as you would furniture, although a sealer coat of varnish is helpful to protect against spills. If you do apply varnish as a sealer, rub the entire bench down between coats with either 400 grade silicon carbide paper or 0000 steel wool, to flatten the nibs on the finish (see page 98). Thin the varnish slightly to help keep it flatter and make it easier to apply.

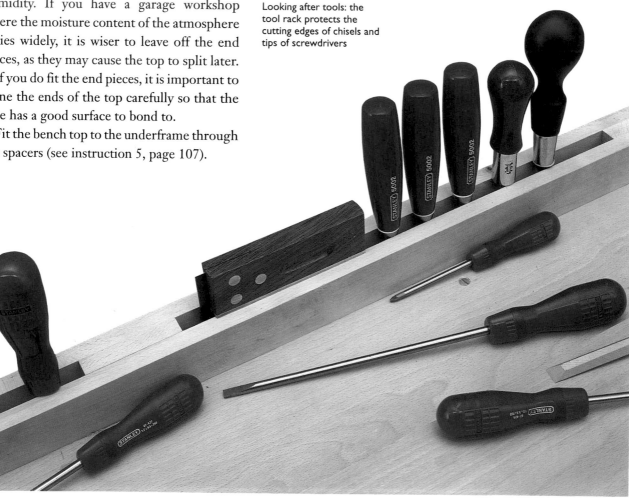

Looking after tools: the tool rack protects the cutting edges of chisels and tips of screwdrivers

CUTTING LIST

COMPONENT	NUMBER	LENGTH in	LENGTH mm	WIDTH in	WIDTH mm	THICKNESS in	THICKNESS mm	COMMENTS
Top	1	60	1520	22¾	580	1⅝–1¾	42	Made up of 4 pieces edge jointed together
length includes 2 end pieces 3½in (90mm) wide								
Tool well bottom	1	60	1520	7	180	¾	20	
Top supports	2	20	510	4	100	¾	20	
Tool well back	1	60	1520	4⅛	105	⅝	15	
Tool rack	1	60	1520	2⅞	72	⅝	15	
Tool well spacers	4	2⅞	72	2⅞	72	⅝	15	
Legs	4	32¼	820	3¾	95	2¾	70	
End frame rails	4	20½	521	3	75	1⅝	40	Including tenons
Back top rail	1	46¼	1170	5½	140	1⅝	40	
Front and back bottom rails	2	46¼	1170	5⅛	130	1⅝	40	

IMPORTANT: HOW TO USE THE WORKING DRAWINGS AND CUTTING LISTS

The drawings and cutting lists should be used in conjunction with the step-by-step instructions for each project.

THE WORKING DRAWINGS

HATCHED AREAS Pieces of wood, or components that are shown in section (i.e., sliced through).

DOTTED LINES Show outlines and positions of components such as joints or rails that are important but would not normally be visible.

CENTER LINES (one short dash and one long one) Show where the center of a cylindrical object (such as a turning) or where a component is symmetrical (i.e., in two mirrored halves). For clarity, individual screws may not be shown but their position will be marked using center lines.

SCALES The original drawings were prepared to scale, but because of a reduction in their size, and because of slight distortions that may occur during printing, these scales are not reproduced here. Instead, the drawings have been fully dimensioned to help you work more easily.

DETAILS Specific moldings or profiles which may be small and unclear on the working drawing have been enlarged and are shown separately.

CUTTING LISTS

The cutting lists identify all the pieces of wood you need to make the furniture. They play an important part in outlining how each project is made. You should never order the wood for a piece of furniture without first understanding where each piece goes. You can check this by following the step-by-step instructions, the photographs and the drawings.

BOOKCASE

This bookcase is constructed in pine, which is a soft material when compared with dense timbers such as oak. It is an easy timber to work with and finish.

HOW TO MAKE THE BOOKCASE
STEP-BY-STEP

1 EDGE JOINTING AND PLANING THE WIDE BOARDS

The sides, top, bottom and shelves of the bookcase are each joined up from two pieces of wood, edge jointed together and planed flat (see page 75). Once you have joined them up, allowing extra for trimming to size, you need to prepare them for marking and cutting the joints.

2 THE CARCASE

The bookcase carcase consists of two solid sides, two shelves and a bottom. It has a back constructed of bead and butt boarding, which is a ready-bought wooden wainscoting with a bead running down one edge. This is held in a rabbet on the back rails and sides. There is also a molded top front rail which will prevent the top front edges of the sides from cupping outward. This rail will also provide an attachment point for the top.

All these separate components make up the main body of the bookcase, and should be made first, before the top and the plinth.

3 MAKING THE CARCASE

The main joints used for the carcase are stopped barefaced dado joints (see page 79) and these hold the shelves and bottom in place. Mark the positions of the joints and clearly show the waste.

The front rails of the carcase will be held in place with stub tenons (see page 77): mark their positions.

The top and bottom rails are held in place with half-lap joints: you should mark the shoulder lines of all these components at this stage to guarantee that all shelves and rails match each other in length.

Next cut and fit the joints.

Bookcase plinth showing glue blocks and plinth supports

4 PROFILING THE EDGES

First cut out any curved edges using a coping saw and then clean them up before shaping (see page 29). Running down the two outside front edges of the sides and along the front edge of the base is a quirk bead. The edges of each shelf and the top front rail are ovolo molded. These profiles soften the edges, stop them being damaged and enhance the overall look of the piece. It is best to form these moldings using a small electric router with a bearing bit, as a combination plane will have difficulty following the cut-out section of the top front rail. If you do not have an electric router use a combination plane for the straight edges and a scratch stock for those that are curved (see page 71).

5 FITTING THE BACK

You should now be left with the basic carcase for the bookcase. Glue the carcase together and cut the bead and butt wainscoting to length to fit into the rabbets in the back rails and sides. (Hold the wainscoting in place with two thin cover strips and screw into position.) Use wood screws to fasten every second or third board to the shelves from behind, as this will keep the back rigid and will remove any slight gaps between them and the back of the shelves. You may prefer to seal the wood prior to gluing (see page 95) to remove any chance of white glue markings appearing on the wood later. If so, make sure all the joints fit, so there is a minimum of cleaning up to do later.

6 MAKING AND FITTING THE TOP

Once the cabinet work for the carcase is complete, trim the top to size, finishing off the edges with a smoothing plane. Round the front corners and then sand them ready for shaping. It is important that these edges are not left rough before putting on the ovolo profile, because any tool used for shaping will follow the slightest undulation on the edge and the finished result will be poor.

The top should overhang about ⅜in (10mm) at the back and about ⅝in (15mm) at the front and sides. Hold it in place with stretcher plates (see above). These will allow the top to expand or contract if it needs to.

7 MAKING THE PLINTH

The plinth is made up as a separate component from the carcase and is screwed in place through blocks from below. Use miters at the two front corners (see page 73) and butt joints at the back (see page 75). Glue blocks strengthen the joints (see page 75). The top front edge and both sides of the plinth have a decorative double ovolo profile – there is no need to continue this around the back edge. Cut out the front of the plinth with a coping saw so it matches the top rail of the bookcase carcase. It too has an ovolo profile.

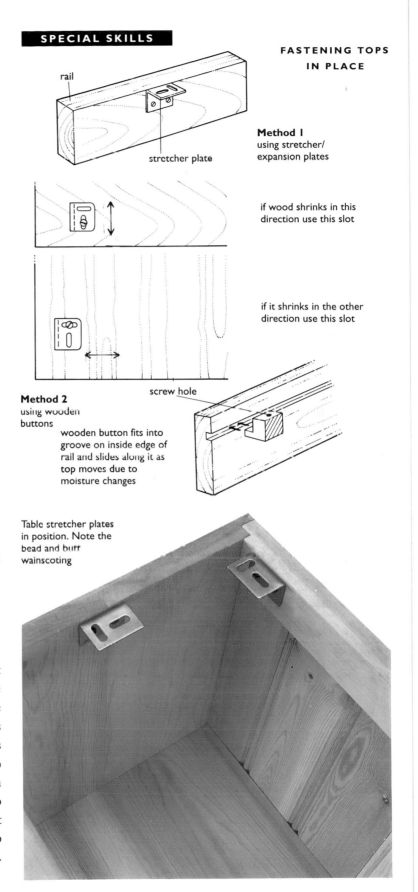

FASTENING TOPS IN PLACE

rail

stretcher plate

Method 1
using stretcher/ expansion plates

if wood shrinks in this direction use this slot

if it shrinks in the other direction use this slot

screw hole

Method 2
using wooden buttons

wooden button fits into groove on inside edge of rail and slides along it as top moves due to moisture changes

Table stretcher plates in position. Note the bead and butt wainscoting

WORKING DRAWINGS

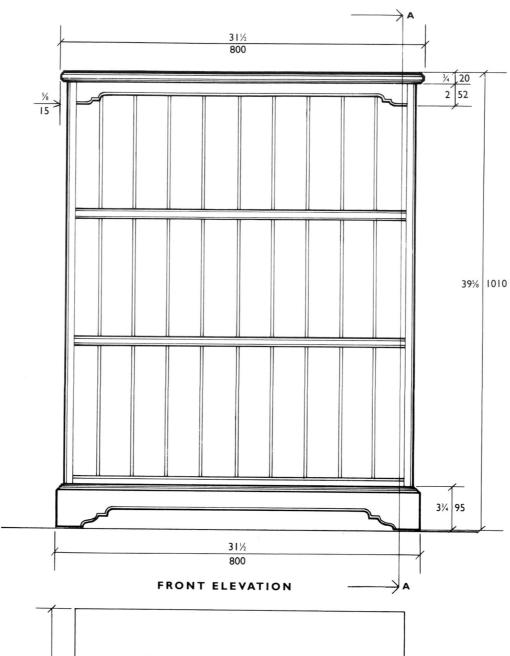

FRONT ELEVATION

DETAIL OF PLINTH MOLDING

NOTE Inches are always shown above and to the left of the line; millimeters always appear below and to the right of the line. Do not mix both sets of measurements

SIDE ELEVATION IN SECTION A–A

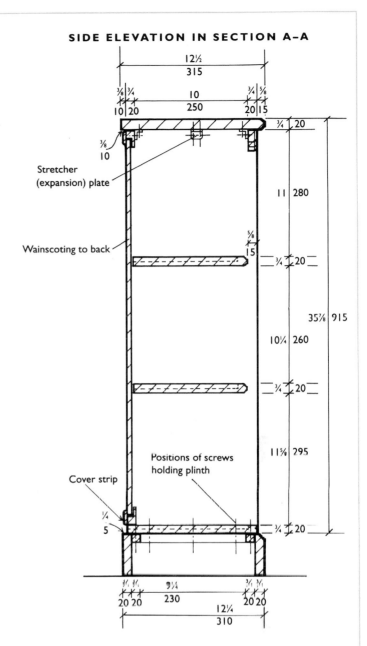

Stretcher (expansion) plate

Wainscoting to back

Positions of screws holding plinth

Cover strip

SECTION THROUGH BOOKCASE SIDE
(on the line of a dado joint)

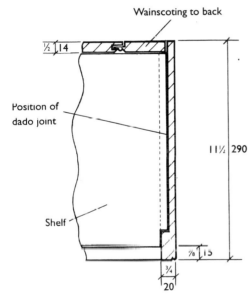

Wainscoting to back

Position of dado joint

Shelf

SECTION THROUGH BACK

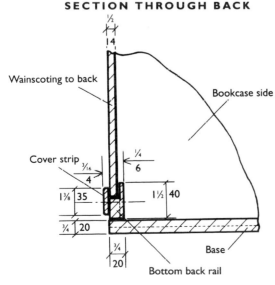

Wainscoting to back

Cover strip

Bookcase side

Base

Bottom back rail

DETAIL OF WAINSCOTING

Amount of wainscot seen when fitted (lay measure)

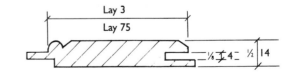

Lay 3
Lay 75

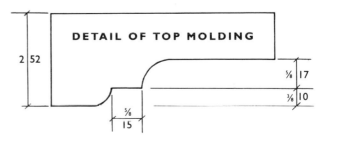

DETAIL OF TOP MOLDING

8 MAKING THE DECORATIVE CUT-OUTS

Mark the cut-outs on to the wood using a template made of thin card or hardboard. Mark the waste and cut it out using a coping saw: this way, the curves will not cause a problem, as the saw blade will easily be able to follow very tight bends.

After removing the waste, clean up the saw marks. I find that sharp broad chisels and round or half-round files produce an acceptable, smooth surface prior to profiling an edge. With care, you could also use a Stanley Surform (see page 36).

9 SANDING

You can glue up the plinth prior to sanding if you wish as all external parts are easily accessible, but with the main carcase, it is better to sand each piece of wood first (especially internal faces) before gluing up. Start sanding on a coarse/medium grit of garnet paper, such as 80/100, and use intermediate papers (e.g. 120 and 150 grade) as necessary, finishing on 180 grade garnet paper (see page 92).

10 FINISHING

Good choices of finish for a pine bookcase include an oil finish (see page 96); or sanding sealer and wax polish (see page 97); or French polish/modified French polish and wax, applied in the same way as sanding sealer (see page 97).

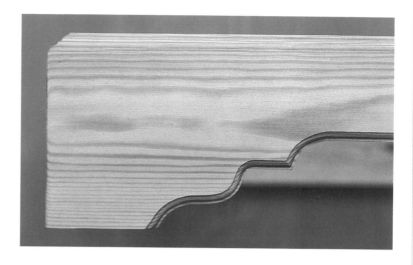

Profile of bookcase plinth with single ovolo mold. Double ovolo mold on the top edge

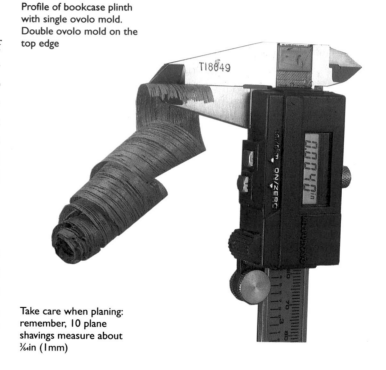

Take care when planing: remember, 10 plane shavings measure about 3/64in (1mm)

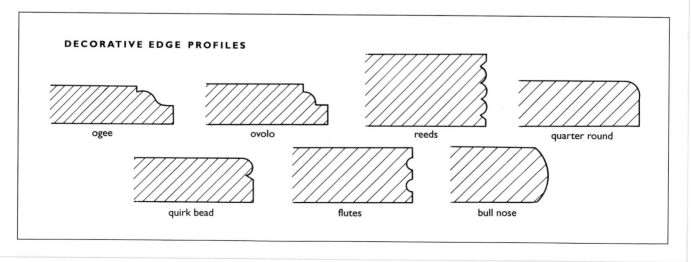

DECORATIVE EDGE PROFILES

ogee

ovolo

reeds

quarter round

quirk bead

flutes

bull nose

CUTTING LIST

COMPONENT	NUMBER	LENGTH in	LENGTH mm	WIDTH in	WIDTH mm	THICKNESS in	THICKNESS mm	COMMENTS
Top	1	31½	800	12½	315	¾	20	Joined from 2 pieces
Shelves	2	29½	750	10⅜	261	¾	20	Joined from 2 pieces
Base	1	29½	750	11½	290	¾	20	Joined from 2 pieces
Sides	2	35⅛	895	11½	290	¾	20	Joined from 2 pieces
Top back rail	1	29½	750	1½	40	¾	20	
Bottom back rail	1	29½	750	1½	40	¾	20	
Front top rail	1	29½	750	2	52	¾	20	
Bead and butt wainscoting made up of 10 pieces ½in (14mm) thick by 3in (75mm) lay measure								
Plinth – front	1	31½	800	3¾	95	¾	20	
Plinth – sides	2	12¼	310	3¾	95	¾	20	
Plinth – back	1	30	760	3¾	95	¾	20	
Back cover strips	2	29¾	755	1⅜	35	3/16	4	
Glue blocks		¾	20	¾	20			From scrap
Plinth supports 8′0″ 2.4m				¾	20	¾	20	

CHILD'S DESK

All the ash veneered MDF required for this piece of furniture can be cut from one standard sheet measuring 96×48×¾in (2440×1220×19mm). The desk is suitable for a child aged 8–12 years.

BASIC SKILLS	
CUTTING SHEET MATERIALS	11
LAYOUT	62
CUTTING AND FITTING MITERS	73
CUTTING AND FITTING DADO JOINTS	79
LAYING OUT AND CUTTING DOVETAILS	80
GLUING UP	83
SANDING	90
BASIC FINISHING	94
FITTING HINGES	142
MAKING A DRAWER	150
SPECIAL SKILLS	
WORKING IN SHEET MATERIALS	125
CUTTING GROOVES	125

All sheet materials have advantages and disadvantages. Here we have chosen MDF but you may decide to work instead in plywood, blockboard or chipboard. These are some pros and cons to bear in mind.

	MDF*	PLYWOOD	BLOCKBOARD	CHIPBOARD
FOR	Produces good crisp edges and will take stains and finishes. Available with decorative veneers on both faces. Screws and glues easily	Stable board, easy to work	A good sheet material to work with, available with a decorative veneer on both faces	Economically priced sheet material, readily available
AGAINST	Difficult to work with hand tools. Saws must have hardpoint teeth. The grooves here are best formed with a small electric router or by lipping all edges and grooving these with a combination plane. Produces irritant dust so wear suitable protection when sanding	Not usually available as a decorative veneered board thicker than ¾in (18mm)	Edges need lipping and end grain of core will not hold screws. Grooving can be difficult when working across the grain with hand tools	Core of chipboard can be quite coarse causing difficulty with screws and glue. Difficult to work with hand tools. Traditional techniques can result in quite weak joints

*Medium Density Fiberboard

HOW TO MAKE THE DESK
STEP-BY-STEP

When working with sheet materials, all edges should be lipped

2 MAKING THE PEDESTAL

The pedestal is the part of the desk containing the shelves. Join the two shelves and base to the sides using stopped, barefaced dado joints, which are strong and also give more rigidity to the carcase (see page 79). Form a ¼in (6mm) groove running down the back inside face of the sides, and along the base, to hold the plywood back. Make a small top back rail, also with a groove, to hold the plywood at the top. This slides into place after gluing the pedestal. Under the base there is a small plinth, which is housed in position. Mark out and cut all the joints for the pedestal before progressing on to the rest of the desk.

The plywood back being slid into position

1 PREPARING THE MDF (MEDIUM DENSITY FIBERBOARD)

First mark out each component on the full sheet of MDF in pencil (see cutting list, page 129). Allow for the width of your saw cut plus a little extra in case you wander from the line. When you are sawing sheet materials, there is a risk that the underside may tear out, so take extra care (see pages 11 and 27). Once you have cut out each piece, square the edges accurately using hand planes (see page 69), and lip all important edges ready for jointing. This includes back edges too, especially if you are to use a combination plane to work the groove.

IMPORTANT

To save money, the shelves, being hidden, can be made of either unveneered MDF, chipboard or plywood lipped to match the ash MDF at the front. These are not allowed for in the layout of the full sheet of MDF.

The child's desk with all the components made and ready for fitting

3 CREATING THE KNEEHOLE

The area of desk where the child sits is called the kneehole. This is formed on one side by the pedestal, and on the other by a simple upright panel. Both sets of uprights – the pedestal and the panel – are housed into the top, and you must allow for this extra when working out the initial measurements. The small drawer (see page 150), slides on a single piece of ash veneered MDF, which is housed into place and provides extra rigidity and support for the kneehole. At the back of the kneehole cut the grooves to hold the gently curved infill panel. This is fastened to the pedestal and to the single upright, again to create a stronger construction (see Special Skill, page 125).

> **TIP**
> To prevent sagging, always store sheet materials flat and never propped upright. Cut to size before storing if necessary.

4 MAKING THE TOP

Make up the top in two parts. The lower part is fixed to the base with stopped dado joints (see page 79). Split the upper part of the top into two and lip it where the two pieces meet. The left-hand side will later be hinged to create a drawing board which tilts into three positions. The fixed flat top at the right-hand side is ideal for making notes, storing papers or to hold an adjustable lamp for studying. This is held in place with wood glue and by screwing from underneath. Cut the recesses for the tilt positions of the top by carefully laying out and cutting with a chisel. Clean up with a router plane.

5 MAKING THE TILT TOP STAYS

There are two tilt top stays, each constructed of a single length of beech or maple. Drill them at one end to hold a steel dowel. Hold this dowel in place in turn with two small pieces of beech or maple, similarly drilled. Glue these to the recess in the underside of the drawing board.

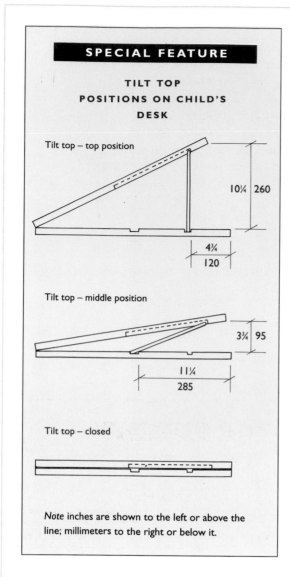

SPECIAL FEATURE

TILT TOP POSITIONS ON CHILD'S DESK

Tilt top – top position

10¼ | 260

4¾
120

Tilt top – middle position

3¾ | 95

11¼
285

Tilt top – closed

Note inches are shown to the left or above the line; millimeters to the right or below it.

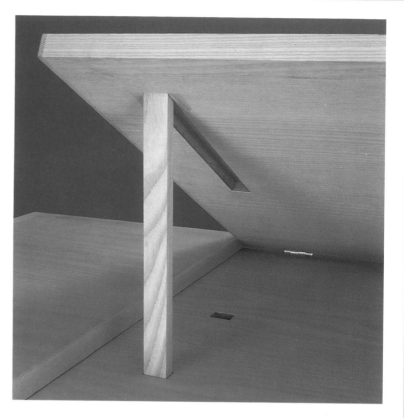

Close-up view of tilt top stays

6 GLUING UP

After careful sanding, you can glue the pedestal, including the plywood back. Leave this to dry and then glue it to the single upright panel, the drawer support, the back panel, and the lower part of the top. This will create the complete carcase to which the drawing board can be fitted.

7 MAKING THE DRAWER

The drawer should really be considered as a shallow tray, although you still construct it using traditional drawer-making techniques (see page 150). It does not need any separate runners, kickers or guides as these are all taken care of by the carcase and top.

8 FITTING THE DRAWING BOARD

The left-hand upper part of the top forms the drawing board. Glue the tilt top stays into position first, before fitting a single pair of hinges at the front to provide a pivot point (see page 142 on fitting hinges). After fitting the drawing board, put the small fixed top into position. Check and plane the edges of this to create a good fit with the lower part of the top. Glue and screw it into place. Sand and finish.

9 FINISHING

A good, quick finish for this desk is to apply two or three coats of clear satin acrylic varnish. This should be rubbed down between coats (see page 98). Being coarse-textured, ash is best denibbed using a fine abrasive webbed pad or flour paper (see page 99) so that small particles do not become caught in the grain. To produce a silkier feel to the surface of the wood, you can rub the last coat of varnish down with the abrasive pad and apply a very small amount of clear paste wax, rubbed well in with a soft cloth.

WORKING IN SHEET MATERIALS

We know that solid wood is prone to warping or splitting as it dries out or readjusts to new surroundings (see page 11). This is why the secondary conditioning of solid wood is so important. Solid wood has another drawback too, in that to make up wide panels and tops, you need considerable time and some skill to edge joint boards together and then accurately plane them smooth again. MDF, and other sheet materials (see page 17) provide an alternative, ready-made flat, stable base. Since they can have a thin layer of decorative veneer glued to them already, all that you have to do is simply cut out the shapes or profiles you need and assemble them using similar methods to knock-down furniture.

However, it is not quite as simple as it sounds. When you are working with sheet materials, there are two very important considerations. The first is that it is vital to strengthen the construction.

If you take a cardboard box and try to push together two opposite corners of the box, the rigidity given by the bottom will stop the box easily folding up. If you take out the bottom of the box, the rigidity is lost. Therefore, when designing furniture in sheet materials, you must always strengthen the carcase, either by boxing in the back rigidly, or by using some form of triangular configuration across its corners to try to stiffen the framework.

On this child's desk, a plywood back is glued into grooves behind the shelves on the pedestal to add strength. A piece of MDF is also housed into the knee-hole area of the desk and is glued in place. This will offer much-needed support, especially to the solitary upright desk side, which is particularly vulnerable to being kicked.

The second problem with working in sheet materials is that edges usually need lipping in some way – a real give-away for antique furniture lovers! You can use iron-on edgings but these tend to peel off or become damaged over quite a short period of time. On this desk, quite wide pieces of wood (½–1⅛in (12–30mm)) have been used as edgings. This width allows for the edges to be easily cleaned up, profiled (or grooved) if necessary and finished. It also helps with any reshaping or refinishing if the edges are accidentally damaged during the lifetime of the furniture.

Apply wide edgings such as these using the same technique as edge jointing boards (see page 75), planing the lipping to exact size later. Be careful not to spill glue on the veneer, or to damage the face veneer during planing.

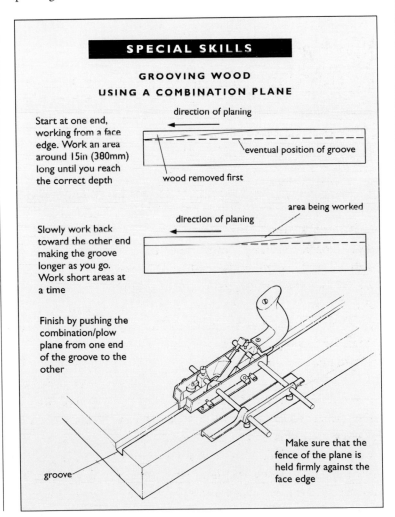

GROOVING WOOD USING A COMBINATION PLANE

Start at one end, working from a face edge. Work an area around 15in (380mm) long until you reach the correct depth

direction of planing

eventual position of groove

wood removed first

Slowly work back toward the other end making the groove longer as you go. Work short areas at a time

direction of planing

area being worked

Finish by pushing the combination/plow plane from one end of the groove to the other

groove

Make sure that the fence of the plane is held firmly against the face edge

WORKING DRAWINGS

FRONT ELEVATION

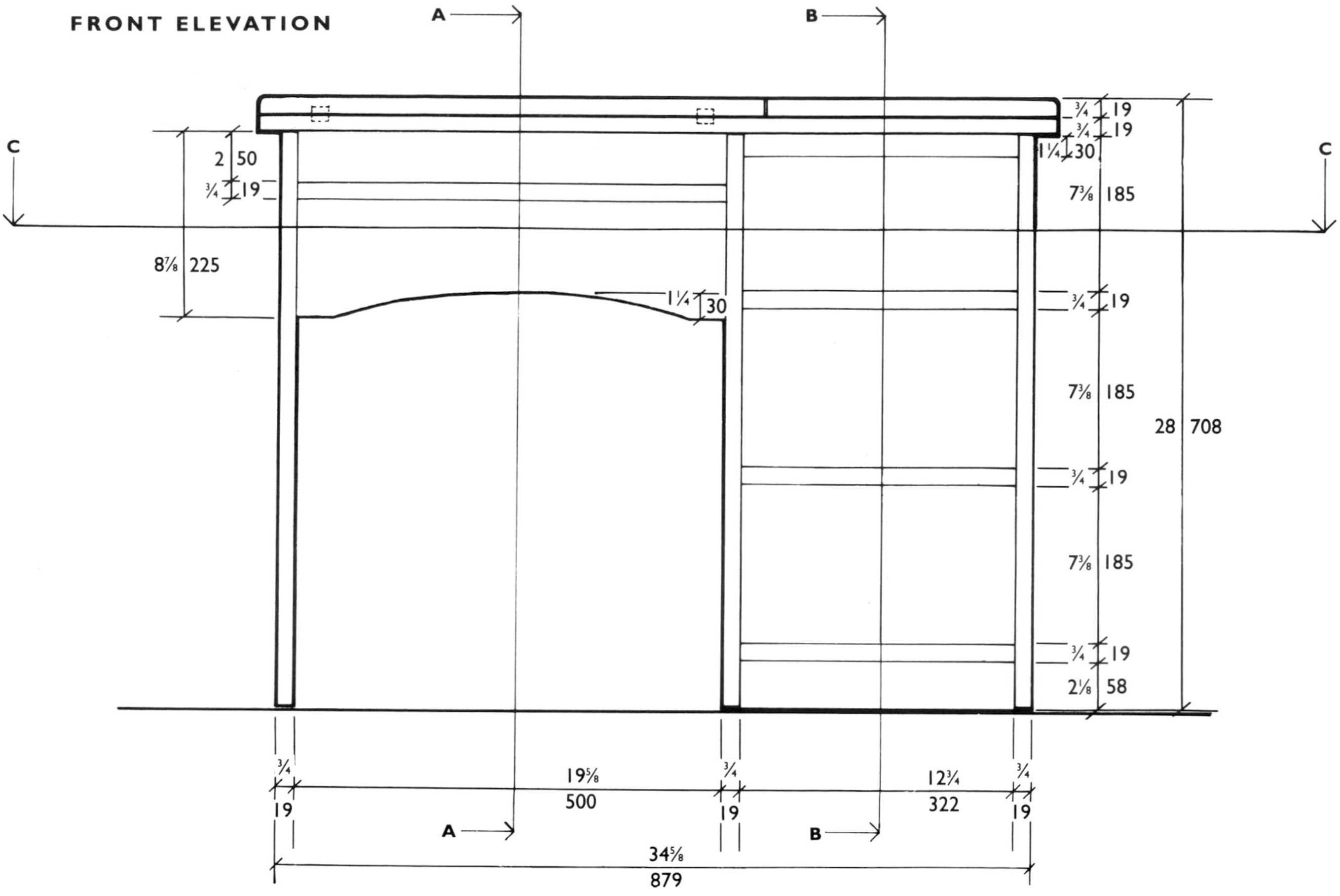
A
B
C
C
2 50
¾ 19
8⅞ 225
1¼ 30
¾ 19
¾ 19
1¼ 30
7⅜ 185
¾ 19
7⅜ 185
28 708
¾ 19
7⅜ 185
¾ 19
2⅛ 58
¾
19
19⅝
500
¾
19
12¾
322
¾
19
A
B
34⅝
879

PLAN-SECTION C–C

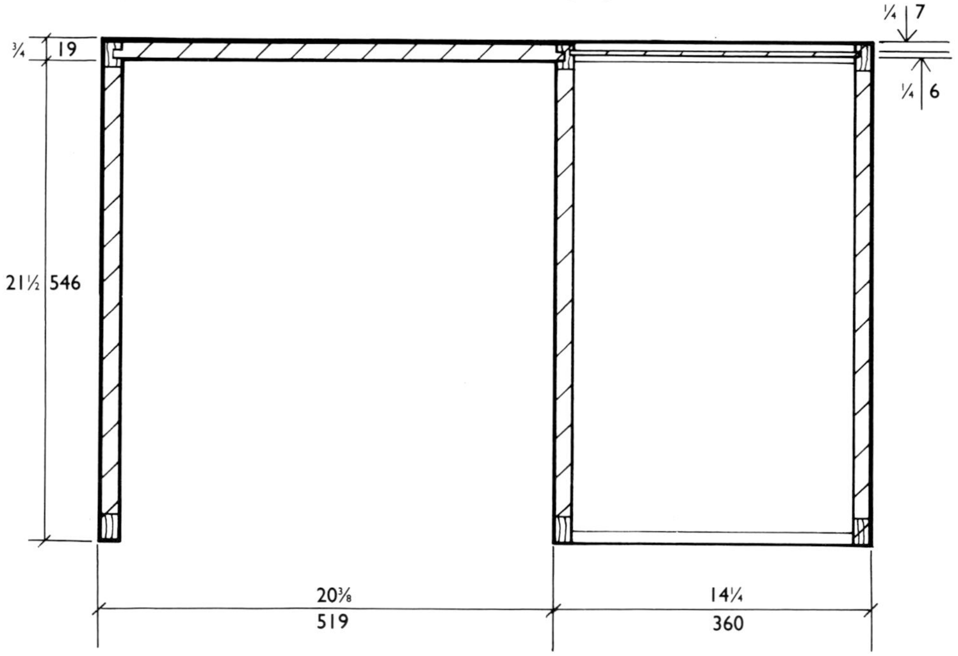
¼ 7
¾ 19
¼ 6
21½ 546
20⅜
519
14¼
360

SIDE ELEVATION A – A IN SECTION

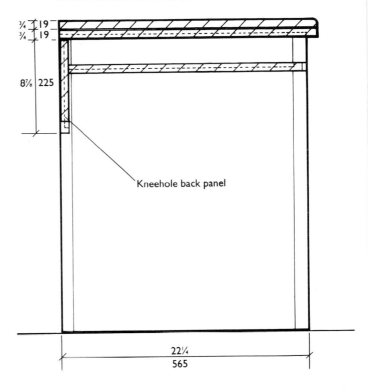

Kneehole back panel

¾ 19
¾ 19
8⅞ 225

22¼
565

SIDE ELEVATION IN SECTION B–B

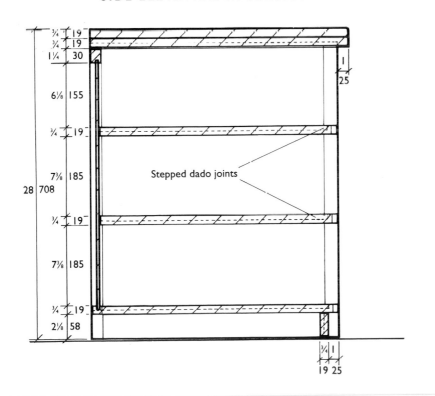

Stepped dado joints

¾ 19
¾ 19
1¼ 30
1
25
6⅛ 155
¾ 19
7⅜ 185
28 708
¾ 19
7⅜ 185
¾ 19
2⅛ 58
¾ 1
19 25

NOTE Inches are always shown above and to the left of the line; millimeters always appear below and to the right of the line. Do not mix both sets of measurements

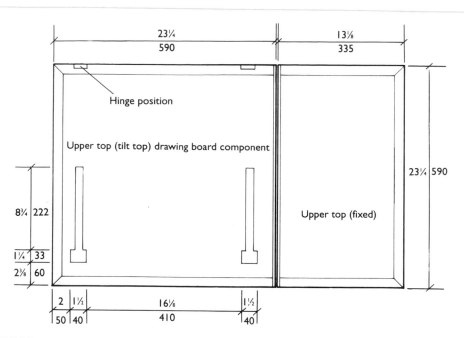

DETAIL OF UNDERSIDE OF UPPER TOP SHOWING TILT TOP POSITIONS

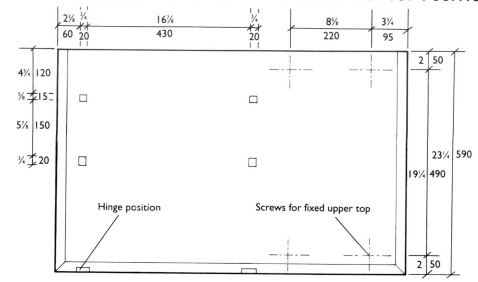

DETAIL OF LOWER TOP

DETAIL IN PLAN – SECTION THROUGH KNEEHOLE AND PEDESTAL

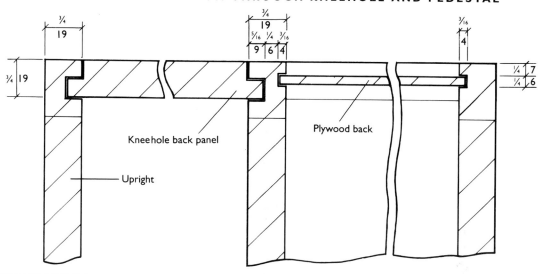

CUTTING LIST

COMPONENT	NUMBER	LENGTH in	LENGTH mm	WIDTH in	WIDTH mm	THICKNESS in	THICKNESS mm	COMMENTS
One 96 × 48 × ¾in (2440 × 1220 × 19mm) sheet of ash veneered Medium Density Fiberboard cuts:	1							***Note* sizes shown are for each complete component. Deduct width of lippings before cutting MDF to size.**
Uprights	3	26⅞	680	22¼	565	¾	19	
Upper part of top	1	23¼	590	23¼	590	¾	19	
Upper part of top	1	13⅛	335	23¼	590	¾	19	
Lower part of top	1	36⅜	925	23¼	590	¾	19	
Drawer support	1	20⅜	520	21½	546	¾	19	
Kneehole back panel	1	8⅞	225	20⅜	520	¾	19	
Other components: Plywood panel – back of pedestal	1	22¾	575	13⅛	330	¼	6	Ash plywood
Back top rail to pedestal	1	13¼	334	1¼	30	¾	20	Solid ash
Tilt top stays	2	10	255	¾	20	⅜	10	Ash/Beech/Maple
Drawer front	1	19⅝	500	2	50	¾	20	Solid Ash
Drawer back	1	19⅝	500	1⅜	35	⅜	9	Beech/Maple
Drawer sides	2	15	380	2	50	⅜	9	Beech/Maple
Plywood bottom	1	19⅜	490	14½	367	¼	6	Birch plywood
Miscellaneous lippings All of same thickness varying from ½in (12mm) to 1⅛in (30mm) wide								Solid Ash
Pedestal shelves	2	21½	546	13½	342	¾	19	Chipboard (Lipped)
Pedestal base	1	22¼	565	13½	342	¾	19	Chipboard (Lipped)
Plinth	1	13½	342	2⅛	58	¾	19	Solid Ash

CHEST

This chest is made of pine, and relies on the use of paneling to provide interest and break up its surfaces. It is relatively simple to construct.

HOW TO MAKE THE CHEST
STEP-BY-STEP

I THE CARCASE

The four corners of the carcase are formed by two front and two back uprights. Each front upright has a rabbet on its inside edge (this avoids having to join two pieces together) and a stopped chamfer on its outside corner. The entire construction has five solid fielded panels, three at the front and one at each end. You should join and plane these now, at the same time as making up the carcase.

The framework that holds these panels in place also makes up the main carcase. This is held together by stopped mortise and tenon joints (see page 76). At the back, the top rail is much wider than on the rest of the construction, to accommodate the hinges. The back of the chest is grooved to hold ¼in (6mm) birch veneered plywood: this is readily available and looks similar to pine.

2 FITTING THE PANELS

Once you have made up the framework, mark the edges to be grooved for holding the panels in pencil, to avoid putting a groove down a wrong edge. Always work from the face side to ensure that the grooves line up with each other. (See Special Skill, grooving wood page 125 and Special Skill page 135.)

3 MAKING THE PLINTH

The plinth of the chest has four sides and in essence is the same construction as the pine bookcase (see the instructions on page 115). Cut out and profile the front of the plinth to improve the proportions and style of the piece. As with the bookcase, use both single and double ovolo profiles to soften the look of the edges.

There is one important difference between this plinth and the bookcase, and this involves the fitting of a piece of plywood to the top of the plinth. This will eventually form the bottom of the chest. You will need to position the supporting blocks, which hold the plywood in place, slightly lower down, to produce, in effect, a ¼in (6mm) rabbet into

Underside of plinth showing glue blocks and plinth supports

The plinth and plywood base glued in place

which you fit and glue the plywood. Any slight discrepancy between the plywood and the plinth will be concealed when you fit the main carcase later. Do this by screwing straight through the supporting blocks from below.

4 MAKING THE TOP

The top of the chest is made up of edge jointed boards. After planing it flat, bull-nose its front and ends using a smoothing plane (see page 70). Cut out the back edge slightly to accommodate the decorative hinges and you may also need to round the bottom corner at the back a little to allow the lid to be lifted without it binding on the main carcase. Slotted bearers will help keep the top flat.

5 DOUBLE-CHECKING

Check each panel for an accurate fit and dry clamp the chest, checking for any joints that may need adjusting. If the chest is to be stained and finished, it is important to check that everything fits; dismantle it, sand and then stain and part-finish, before gluing up. If the wood is to be left natural, sand and just part-finish the panels before fitting.

6 GLUING UP

Glue the carcase first. Glue the two end panels, and leave to dry. Next, glue the front and back to the end panels. Make absolutely sure that any glue from the mortise and tenon joints that accidentally spills on the panels during gluing does not restrict the panels from moving due to moisture changes. Glue the plinth together next.

7 FITTING THE PLINTH

Fit the plinth by simply screwing from below through the supporting blocks. Ensure that the plinth protrudes a uniform distance from the carcase at the front and sides.

The two front corner uprights have stopped chamfers as features and to prevent them being damaged

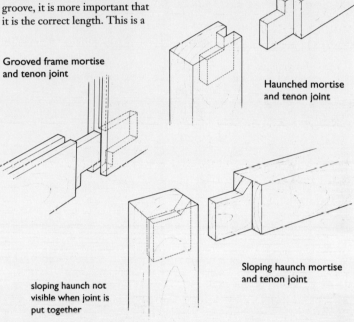

SPECIAL SKILLS

Tenons at the corners of rectangular frames often need to be 'inset' from the end so that the joint looks neat but still has enough strength. This can be achieved by haunching the joint to give the tenon more width.

Haunches are also used to fill in grooves that run from one end of a piece of wood to the other. It is common for the haunch to be as long as it is wide, although where it is used to fill in a groove, it is more important that it is the correct length. This is a grooved frame mortise and tenon joint. On important ends, where the groove does not run all the way through and a haunch is preferable for strength, it is best to use a sloping haunch which will not be visible. Haunching a joint has the added benefit that when cleaning up the mortise, there is less chance of damaging the shoulder when pulling back on the chisel.

Grooved frame mortise and tenon joint

Haunched mortise and tenon joint

sloping haunch not visible when joint is put together

Sloping haunch mortise and tenon joint

Back of chest showing the wide top back rail holding the hinge in place

8 FITTING THE TOP

The top is simple to fit. Fasten the hinges in place before finishing to check that they are correctly positioned. Next, remove them, en-suring that you can see the holes clearly. Finish polishing the chest and then refit the hinges in their original position. This will guarantee that there is no chance of damaging the surface of the chest while fitting the hinges.

9 FINISHING

The most suitable finishes for this chest are satin polyurethane or satin acrylic varnish (two to three coats finished with a light waxing of white/clear furniture paste wax will give a silky feel (see page 98)); for a satin sheen, but with less protection, use sanding sealer and wax (see page 97); or, for a simple, low-luster effect, an oil finish (see page 96).

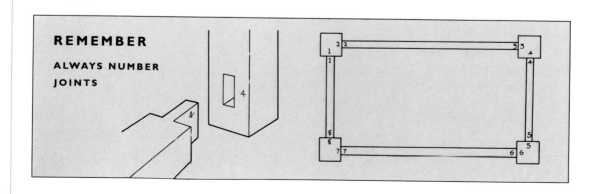

REMEMBER

ALWAYS NUMBER JOINTS

MAKING AND FITTING RAISED AND FIELDED PANELS

First you need to produce the framework, laying out and cutting the mortise and tenon joints. This gives you the 'skeleton' of the carcase with 'holes' in the center, which will be infilled with panels – grooves on the internal edges of this 'skeleton' will hold the panels in place.

Decide on the width of the groove needed to hold the panel. With this chest it is ¼in (6mm). If you use a plow plane to cut the grooves (see page 125), they will have to run from one end of the piece of wood to the other. If this is so, the mortise and tenons will need an extension on the shoulder of the tenon (haunching) to fill in the gap left by the groove (see page 133). Always work the grooves from the face side markings to guarantee that they all align.

Make sure you cut the panels wide enough and long enough to fit into the grooves, but do not make them so large that they strain the joints of the framework. You must also avoid making them too small, because if the panels later shrink, gaps will be created.

Generally, overall, the panel should be approximately ⅜–½in (10–13mm) wider and longer than the hole it is filling (³⁄₁₆–¼in (5–6mm) either side), with the groove being ¹⁄₁₆in (1–2mm) deeper than the depth of the tongue on the panel. This produces a comfortable fit. When you are working in solid wood, it is easy to make mistakes that are easily avoidable, but can so often be seen on work involving raised and fielded panels. For example, a panel can often split because it has been fully glued in place. Avoid this by using only a dab of glue at the top and bottom center of the panel to hold it at the center of the framework. This will allow the wood to expand or contract from the middle.

TYPES OF PANEL

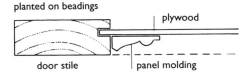

planted on beadings
plywood
door stile
panel molding

Panel molding: lies below surface of stile

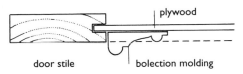

plywood
door stile
bolection molding

Bolection molding: stands proud of surface of stile

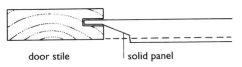

door stile
solid panel

Raised and fielded panel

Note a sunk panel is one where its face lies below that of the surrounding framework

A further, very noticeable, problem, concerns the positioning of the panels themselves. It is vital that they are fitted into the frame correctly. You can make a better job of this if you ensure the panel has a proper square tongue running all around its outside edge, allowing it to fit snugly into the groove. The tongue should preferably not be tapered because it will then sit in one position only. Sometimes (as on the molding of the raised and fielded panels on this chest) you will have no choice: here, modern router cutters, designed specifically for sheet materials, have been used. In this case, careful fitting and the use of correctly dried wood are of paramount importance.

BEWARE

One mistake often to be seen on stained panels is where the panel shrinks, exposing white wood. When you are staining, it is best to stain and part finish the panel before assembly, so that when it moves, as it probably will, no light-colored wood will become visible.

MAKING A RAISED AND FIELDED PANEL BY HAND

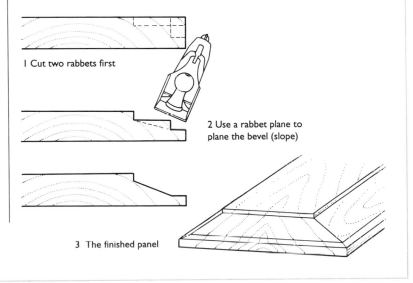

1 Cut two rabbets first

2 Use a rabbet plane to plane the bevel (slope)

3 The finished panel

WORKING DRAWINGS

FRONT ELEVATION

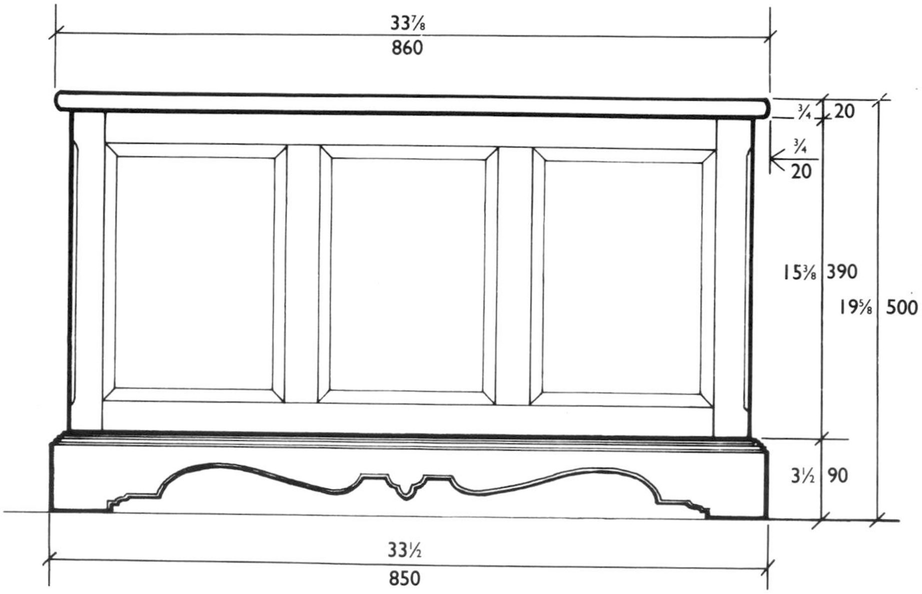
33⅞
860
¾ 20
¾
20
15⅜ 390
19⅝ 500
3½ 90
33½
850

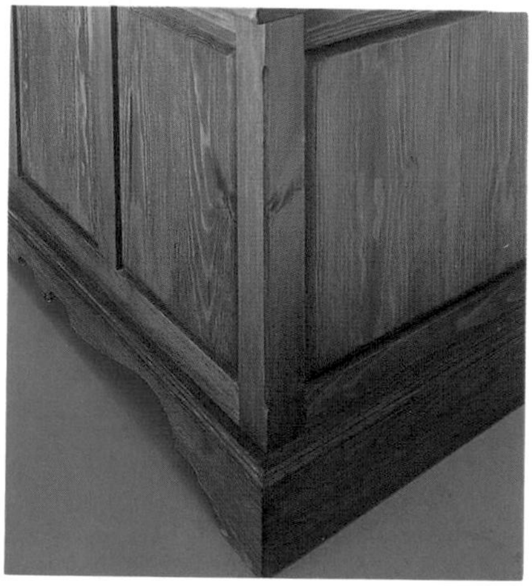

NOTE Inches are always shown above and to the left of the line; millimeters always appear below and to the right of the line. Do not mix both sets of measurements

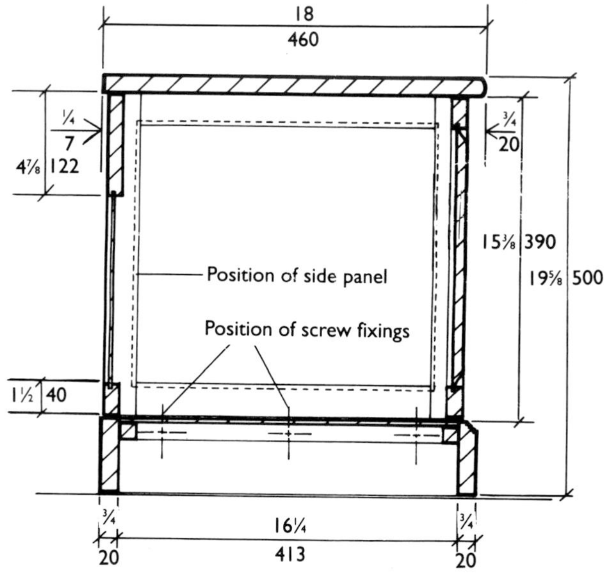
18
460
¼
7
4⅞ 122
¾
20
15⅜ 390
19⅝ 500
Position of side panel
Position of screw fixings
1½ 40
¾
20
16¼
413
¾
20

SIDE ELEVATION IN SECTION

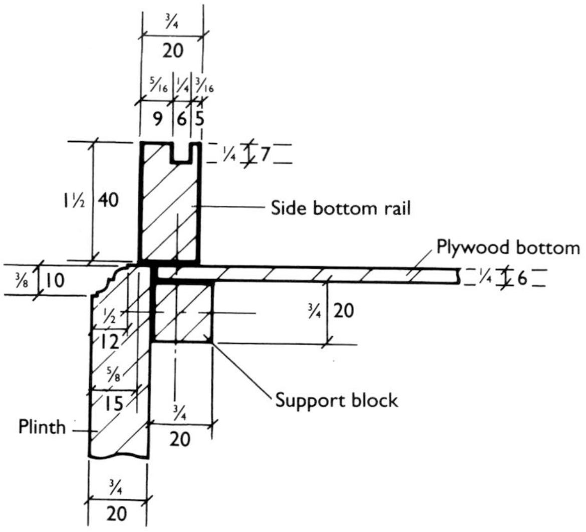
¾
20
5⁄16 ¼ 3⁄16
9 6 5
¼ 7
1½ 40
Side bottom rail
Plywood bottom
⅜ 10
¼ 6
½
12
¾ 20
⅝
15
Support block
Plinth
¾
20
¾
20

DETAIL OF SECTION THROUGH PLINTH

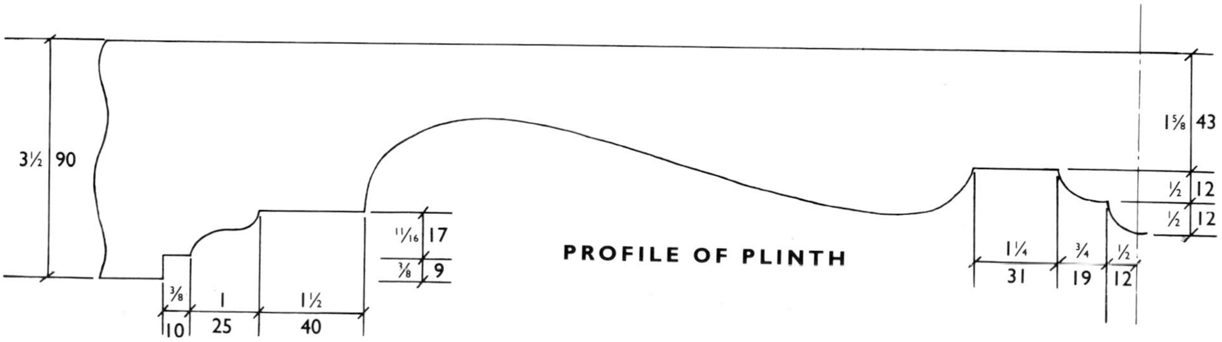
3½ 90
11⁄16 17
⅜ 9
⅜
10
1
25
1½
40
1⅝ 43
½ 12
½ 12
1¼
31
¾
19
½
12

PROFILE OF PLINTH

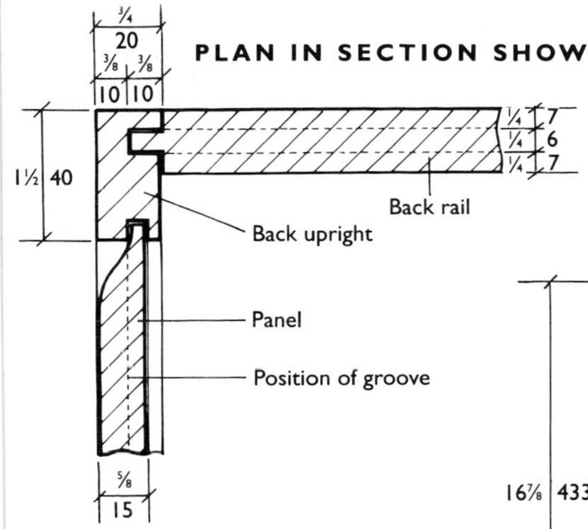
PLAN IN SECTION SHOWING DETAIL OF BACK
Back rail
Back upright
Panel
Position of groove

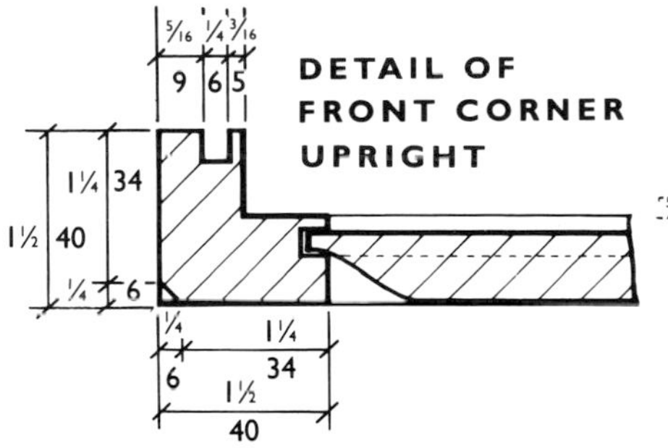
DETAIL OF FRONT CORNER UPRIGHT

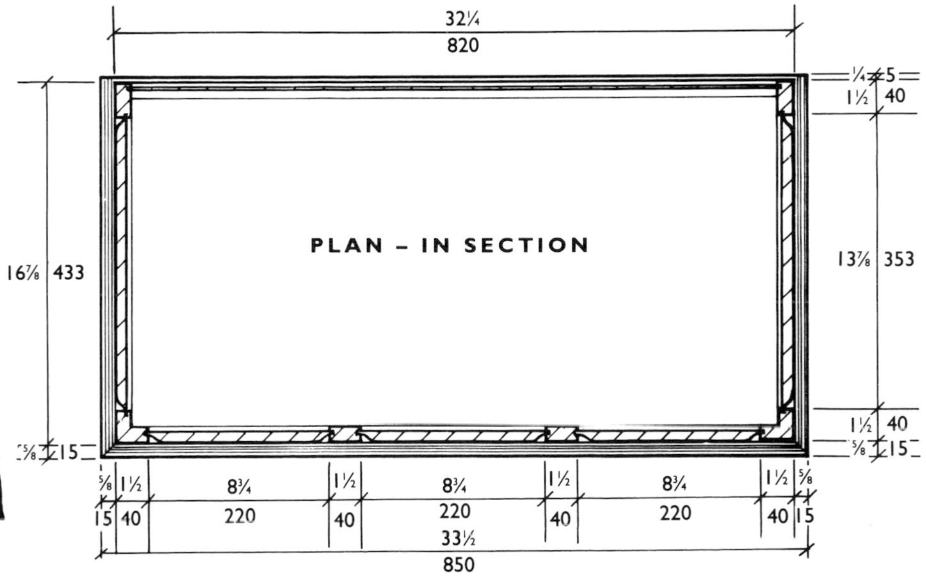
PLAN – IN SECTION
32¼
820
33½
850
16⅞ 433
13⅞ 353

CUTTING LIST

COMPONENT	NUMBER	LENGTH in	LENGTH mm	WIDTH in	WIDTH mm	THICKNESS in	THICKNESS mm	COMMENTS
Top	1	33⅞	860	18	460	¾	20	Made up of 3 pieces edge jointed together
Front uprights	2	15⅜	390	1½	40	1½	40	
Back uprights	2	15⅜	390	1½	40	¾	20	
Side rails top and bottom	4	15⅜	391	1½	40	¾	20	Includes tenons
Front rails top and bottom	2	30¾	782	1½	40	¾	20	Includes tenons
Central mullion	2	13⅞	350	1½	40	¾	20	Includes tenons
Top back rail	1	31½	800	4⅞	122	¾	20	Includes tenons
Bottom back rail	1	31½	800	1½	40	¾	20	Includes tenons
Plywood back	1	9½	240	31¼	792	¼	6	Birch plywood
Plinth – front	1	33½	850	3½	90	¾	20	
Plinth – sides	2	17¾	453	3½	90	¾	20	
Plinth – back	1	32	810	3½	90	¾	20	
Plywood base	1	16¼	413	32¼	820	¼	6	Birch plywood
Plinth supports	2	32	810	¾	20	¾	20	
Plinth supports	4	14¾	373	¾	20	¾	20	
Glue blocks		¾	20	¾	20			Out of scrap
Front panels	3	12⅞	320	9¼	232	⅝	15	Joined up in 2 pieces
Side panels	2	12⅞	320	14⅜	365	⅝	15	Joined up in 2 pieces

BEDSIDE CABINET

This simple cabinet has solid sides, shelf, base and top, all of which involve the techniques of planing boards flat and cutting wide dado joints. This project will also teach you how to fit a door.

HOW TO MAKE THE CABINET

STEP-BY-STEP

1 MAKING THE CARCASE

First, cut and plane the wood to size, and join up the sides, shelf and base (as well as the top). Plane these flat and cut them to size. The shelf and base are fastened into place using stopped barefaced dado joints (see page 79). Next, mark out and cut the back and front top rail. These are secured to the sides using twin stub tenons (see opposite).

Groove the back of the cabinet to hold the ¼in (6mm) plywood back. The shelf sits in front of the plywood back and is therefore not grooved.

2 MAKING THE PLINTH

Construct the plinth of this bedside cabinet in the same way as the bookcase plinth (see page 115), except that since this one is wider, it is a good idea to put slots in the supporting blocks to allow for possible expansion and contraction of the base.

3 MAKING THE TOP

Make the top by edge jointing two pieces of wood and after planing flat, trim it to size. Mark the rounds of the two front corners using a can lid as a template and cut them using a coping saw. Smooth them by sanding.

4 THE DECORATION

Ovolo profiles (see page 118) on the two ends and front of the top, on both its top and bottom, match the plinth. Use a quirk bead (see page 118) to decorate the outside front edge of both sides and along the top front edge of the shelf to soften the edges gently.

As the plywood back panel is small, it has been grooved into position. On chests of drawers or large cabinets, it is best to use rabbets and screw through fillets from the back. This will allow access should the drawer swell and be stuck in place

SPECIAL SKILLS

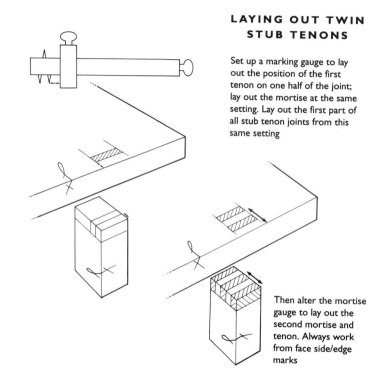

LAYING OUT TWIN STUB TENONS

Set up a marking gauge to lay out the position of the first tenon on one half of the joint; lay out the mortise at the same setting. Lay out the first part of all stub tenon joints from this same setting

Then alter the mortise gauge to lay out the second mortise and tenon. Always work from face side/edge marks

Select good quality
hardware for doors
and drawers to add
the finishing touch

1 Ring handle
2 Drop handles
3 Cabinet handle
4 Flat knob
5 Domed knob
6 Plate handle
7 Escutcheon
8 Fretted plate handle
9 Snake and H hinge
10 Magnetic catch
11 Ball catch
12 Double ball catch

5 MAKING THE DOOR

The next stage is to make the door (see Special Skill page 142). The corner joints of the frame are mortise and tenons. Mark and cut these joints – they will need to be haunched if you cut the grooves using a combination plane (see page 133). For more details on making and fitting the panel, see page 135.

6 SANDING AND GLUING

After making the carcase, plinth, top and door, sand all internal faces. Seal them if you wish, to avoid damage by glue spillage. Next glue the carcase and plinth and fit together.

7 FITTING THE TOP

Hold the top in place by screwing through the top front rail, using stretcher plates at the back to allow the wood to move if it needs to (see page 115).

8 FINISHING

You can create a natural-looking finish by using sanding sealer and paste wax (see page 97), although you may find that this will mark if the furniture is not looked after carefully. If you require extra protection, use a satin polyurethane or a satin acrylic varnish instead (see page 98).

MAKING AND FITTING DOORS

There are several ways to fit doors: this is one simple method that works.

A door is a piece of movable joinery which should fit accurately into its opening. If a door is hung incorrectly, it will either scrape against the sides or bottom, appear lop-sided, or have uneven gaps around its edges.

MAKING THE DOOR

The door itself (when made to a traditional construction rather than merely being cut from man-made sheet materials), consists of a framework of four lengths of wood, mortised and tenoned into each other. The center is infilled with a solid panel held in grooves. As long as it is properly constructed, this sort of framework will keep the door flat and true and allow the panel to expand or contract if it needs to. See page 135 for making the panel.

Use molded grooved frame or molded frame mortise and tenon joints (see pages 77, 133 and 145) on the door of this bedside cabinet, which will accommodate the decorative ovolo profile by being neatly mitered at the corners.

INITIAL FITTING OF THE DOOR

When you have made and assembled the door, true up its bottom edge with a smoothing plane to make it stand perfectly upright. Next make the door fit the carcase on the hinge side by careful planing to make it match the cabinet. Then fit the top and other side of the door, leaving a gap of around ¹⁄₃₂in (0.75mm) between the carcase and the door.

If you feel it helps, you can very slightly bevel the edges of the door toward the back which will assist you in the final fitting.

THE HINGES

Brass butt hinges are the most common type used on traditional doors. They are usually fitted equally into both the door opening and the stile of the door. You may however prefer to fit them into the door only, which is a little easier as you will only have to cut out recesses on the door stile to hold the hinges.

WHERE TO PUT HINGES

There is no fixed rule for the position of hinges. The best rule in fact is the rule of thumb – literally. Put the door on a bench (with the stile parallel to the front of the bench) and put a thumb from each hand an equal distance from the top and bottom edges of the door. If this is obviously too far apart, slowly bring your thumbs together, moving equally until you think you are in the right area. It is simply a matter of judgement, but is generally just less than a quarter of the length of the stile measured from the top or bottom edge of the door. Look at other pieces of furniture around the house if you need guidance.

Allowing for 'creep' when chopping out hinge recesses: move the hinge just over the first knife line before laying out position of the other end of the hinge

HANGING THE DOOR

Fit the hinges to the door first. Put the door frame in a vise and lightly mark the position of the bottom edge of each hinge with a sharp knife, using a square to continue this knife line across the edge of the door stile. Next put the hinge on the door stile so that it just covers this first knife line and lightly mark the position of the top of the hinge with the knife. This small movement of the hinge allows for the creep of the chisel (see page 82) when chopping out the recess. Put two light pencil lines down the front of the stile to show where to stop and start the mortise gauge when laying out the depth of the hinge.

As well as the length, you must also allow for chisel creep on the width and depth of the hinge. To do this set up a marking gauge to a measurement of about ¹⁄₆₄in (0.25mm) less than half the total width of the hinge. Next, set up a second gauge to around ¹⁄₆₄in (0.25mm) less than half of the total thickness of the hinge. Or, more simply, set up each measurement and then reduce it by a tiny fraction.

The best way to establish half the width is to pick up the hinge, open it up fully and measure it accurately. Let's say this equals 1⅛in (28mm). Half of this is ⁹⁄₁₆in (14mm), so set the marking gauge to this measurement, less the amount to be allowed for creep.

You can now use both marking gauges to lay out the positions of the width and the depth of the hinge. Finally, chop out the hinge recess by carefully working back to the gauge lines with a chisel.

Note if you have only one marking gauge, lay out the width first, reset and then lay out the depth.

TIP

When fitting hinges, always fit only one screw at a time, checking that the door still opens and closes in the correct place after each one.

When fitting the door to the carcase, lay out the exact position with a knife to the top or bottom of each hinge only. Lay out the other side (i.e. the length) of the hinge by using the hinge itself as a template, again not forgetting to allow for the creep of the chisel. Use the previously set-up gauges to lay out the width and depth of the hinges and chop out carefully.

The final fit of a door is important, as unsightly gaps or twisted door frames, causing the door to stand proud, are easily seen defects. If you practice and steadily improve your layout accuracy, these will not be frustrating problems.

After finishing, fit door stops and handles as required.

Where two doors meet (looking down) they can butt together or have their edges rabbeted to fit each other

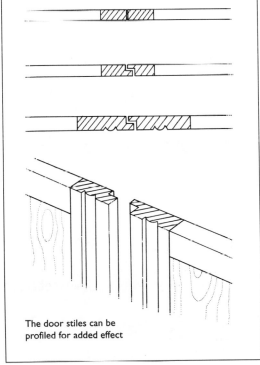

The door stiles can be profiled for added effect

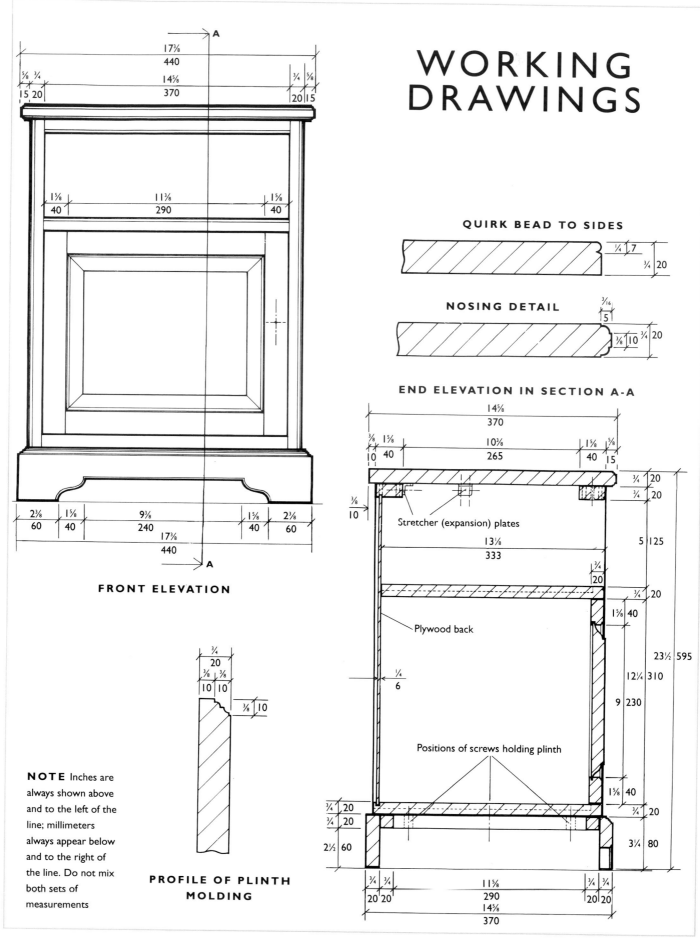

WORKING DRAWINGS

FRONT ELEVATION

QUIRK BEAD TO SIDES

NOSING DETAIL

END ELEVATION IN SECTION A-A

Stretcher (expansion) plates

Plywood back

Positions of screws holding plinth

PROFILE OF PLINTH MOLDING

NOTE Inches are always shown above and to the left of the line; millimeters always appear below and to the right of the line. Do not mix both sets of measurements

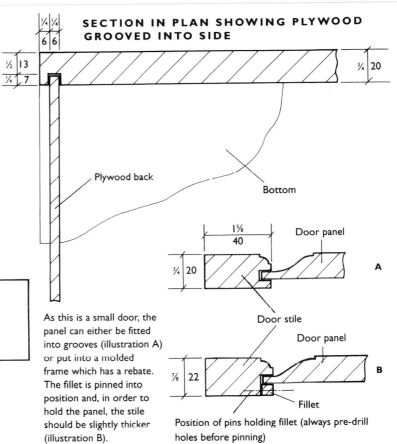

SECTION IN PLAN SHOWING PLYWOOD GROOVED INTO SIDE

Plywood back

Bottom

Door panel

A

Door stile

Door panel

B

Fillet

Position of pins holding fillet (always pre-drill holes before pinning)

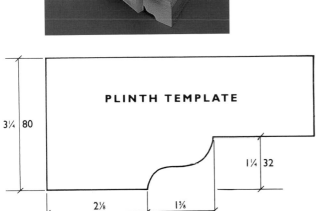

PLINTH TEMPLATE

As this is a small door, the panel can either be fitted into grooves (illustration A) or put into a molded frame which has a rebate. The fillet is pinned into position and, in order to hold the panel, the stile should be slightly thicker (illustration B).

CUTTING LIST

COMPONENT	NUMBER	LENGTH in/mm		WIDTH in/mm		THICKNESS in/mm		COMMENTS
Top	1	$17\frac{3}{8}$	440	$14\frac{5}{8}$	370	$\frac{3}{4}$	20	Made up of 3 pieces edge jointed together
Shelf	1	$15\frac{5}{8}$	390	$13\frac{1}{8}$	333	$\frac{3}{4}$	20	Includes housings. Joined up in 3 pieces
Bottom	1	$15\frac{5}{8}$	390	$13\frac{5}{8}$	345	$\frac{3}{4}$	20	Made up of 3 pieces edge jointed together. Includes housings joined up in 3 pieces
Sides	2	$19\frac{1}{2}$	495	$13\frac{5}{8}$	345	$\frac{3}{4}$	20	
Front and back top rails	2	$15\frac{5}{8}$	390	$1\frac{5}{8}$	40	$\frac{3}{4}$	20	Includes tenons
Plinth – front	1	$17\frac{3}{8}$	440	$3\frac{1}{4}$	80	$\frac{3}{4}$	20	
Plinth – sides	2	$14\frac{5}{8}$	370	$3\frac{1}{4}$	80	$\frac{3}{4}$	20	
Plinth – back	1	$15\frac{7}{8}$	400	$3\frac{1}{4}$	80	$\frac{3}{4}$	20	
Glue blocks				$\frac{3}{4}$	20	$\frac{3}{4}$	20	Out of scrap
Door stiles	2	$12\frac{1}{4}$	310	$1\frac{5}{8}$	40	$\frac{3}{4}$	20	See working drawings reference grooves or rebates
Door rails	2	$12\frac{7}{8}$	330	$1\frac{5}{8}$	40	$\frac{3}{4}$	20	Includes tenons
Door panel	1	$9\frac{1}{2}$	242	$11\frac{7}{8}$	302	$\frac{5}{8}$	15	Joined up in 2 pieces
Plywood back	1	$18\frac{1}{2}$	467	$15\frac{1}{8}$	382	$\frac{1}{4}$	6	Birch plywood

SMALL TABLE WITH DRAWER

This small oak table is straightforward except for the one extra that makes it a little more complicated – namely the drawer. Fitting drawers can separate the amateur from the professional, yet if you follow a basic procedure, with practice you will find that the job is actually quite simple.

HOW TO MAKE THE TABLE
STEP-BY-STEP

1 PREPARING THE CARCASE

Start by cutting and preparing the wood for the carcase: make two front rails, one wide back rail and two wide side rails, as well as four legs and four narrow rails for the bottom.

2 MAKING THE LEGS

The legs on this table are turned on a lathe. Turning is a skill in itself and is not covered in this book: the further reading on page 155 will help. If you do not want to turn the legs yourself you can buy ready-turned legs or substitute the legs for square ones – extra decorations, such as stopped chamfers on the corners or flutes, will help to keep the table in proportion.

Whatever type of leg you choose, first lay out in pencil the positions of the mortise and tenon joints.

3 MAKING THE CARCASE

The joints making up the carcase are simple stopped mortise and tenons (see page 76). As usual, when laying these out, always work from the face side and edge marks – but in this case you will need to reset the stock of your mortise gauge after laying out the tenons to allow for the rails to sit back from the front edge of the legs.

The two sets of twin stub tenons on the top front rails are cut out in the same way as normal tenons, but cut out the waste in the center with a coping saw and clean up with a bevel-edged chisel. This is the same technique used for cutting out waste between the pins on dovetail joints (see pages 42 and 81). After making up the carcase and checking that the joints fit, prepare the top by edge jointing two pieces together (see page 75). Leave to dry and trim to size.

Twin stub tenons: the width of the tenons can be made narrower, creating edge shoulders, as this prevents the mortise being damaged during cutting

---

TIP

If you turn the legs yourself it is a good idea to turn them before cutting the mortises out for the rails: otherwise, the fact that some wood has been removed will increase the chance of the leg vibrating on the lathe as it spins due to centrifugal force.

4 MAKING AND FITTING THE DRAWER CARCASE

This piece of furniture has a traditional drawer supported and steered by runners, kickers and guides – see Special Skill (page 150) for how to mark out, cut, glue, fit and clean up drawers.

5 MAKING THE DECORATIVE EDGES

Lightly round the square corners of the legs except those that meet the two top front rails. Round the four edges of the bottom rails too, but a little more than on the legs.

Work an ovolo profile around the ends and front edge of the top, as well as the bottom outside edge of the back and side rails (see page 118).

6 FITTING A DUST PANEL

You can add an additional touch of quality to furniture by fitting a dust panel. This is simply a plywood panel grooved into the carcase below a drawer. In this case, the plywood fits into the back edge of the bottom front rail and the inside edge of the runners and back rail. A dust panel neatly finishes off the underside of a carcase, and in furniture with multiple drawers, stops objects falling from one drawer into the one below it. Next, glue the carcase together ready for fitting the top.

7 CLEANING AND SANDING

Now clean up the entire work, including the top ends of the legs where the rails are fitted into them. This will guarantee the top sits flush. Next, sand ready for finishing. You can sand, stain and part-finish before gluing if you prefer, or carry out the staining and finishing process later on the fully glued-up project.

8 FITTING THE TOP

Secure the top using wood screws fastened through the top rail. Use stretcher plates, or buttons (see page 115), at the back to allow the top to move due to changes in moisture content.

9 STAINING

Oak may be stained dark to resemble old oak furniture, or you could keep it natural if you prefer. A water-based stain will give the best depth of color and for best results apply the stain with a brush, wiping it off again with a cloth, and never allowing the stain to dry out. Do not forget to raise the grain first (see page 101). A dash of ammonia will help the stain to bite into the wood.

10 FINISHING

For the simplest and most effective finish, apply three to four coats of white or transparent French polish, which dries clear. You could use thinned garnet or button shellac to tone the work if you prefer.

Follow this by waxing the furniture with a soft paste wax to pull out a top quality natural sheen (see page 97).

Dry clamping showing runners, kickers and guides. On large constructions, the top rails can be dovetailed into the sides and blocked out for rigidity. Runners and kickers can then be held in grooves or screwed and glued into place afterwards for ease of fitting

SPECIAL SKILL

MAKING AND FITTING DRAWERS

Drawers are effectively deep trays, sliding in and out of a carcase. This means that to fit one you will have to consider both the drawer and the parts it slides on.

POINTS TO CONSIDER WHEN MAKING THE CARCASE

When making up the carcase, ensure that it is as square as possible. On traditional drawers there are three sets of rails which guide the drawer into place. These are the runners (which the drawer sits on), the kickers, which look similar to the runners except that they run along the top of the drawer sides (preventing the drawer from toppling forward as it is pulled outward), and the guides, which steer the drawer in the carcase. On multiple sets of drawers, say a three-drawer chest, you can make the kicker of one drawer become the runner for the drawer above it.

Join the runners and kickers either into the front and back rails of the carcase or screw and glue to the sides for strength and support. The guides are screwed and glued into place. Even though all three perform totally separate tasks each must run parallel and at the same time be at 90 degrees to the front of the carcase. Otherwise, the drawer will either bind, fit sloppily or even worse, will not open and close properly. If you do find that the carcase is a little out of square, you should still try to make the kickers, guides and runners run as true and accurately as you can.

MAKING THE DRAWER

A drawer is made up of two sides, a front, a back and a bottom. The fronts of most drawers are usually made from a decorative wood, most often the same as the rest of the cabinet. This is usually a little thicker than the sides and back.

Before making the drawer, plane the left and right drawer sides and make them fit exactly their position in the drawer space. Check they slide in and out properly. If you select wood with the grain running toward the back of the drawer you can lightly clean up the sides later in final fitting without damaging the front.

You can either make the length of the back fit the opening exactly, or leave it a little longer on its length to allow for cleaning up (see page 89). If you cut the back exactly to size you must mark out the joints extremely accurately as there will be only a small amount of wood for cleaning up later. Fit the front to width but let the length of the front overhang very slightly. If you really want to be professional, make the ends of the drawer front bevel very slightly inwards so that the drawer front actually fits into the carcase a little before becoming, in effect, wedged in place. Work as accurately as you can. With this method you can carefully take off one or two shavings at a time with a smoothing plane after assembly, as you fit the drawer. Next groove the drawer sides and front (make sure you put the groove where it will be covered by the dovetails see right). Once you know the position of the groove, you can cut and plane the back of the drawer to its correct width.

(see page 89)

TIP
If you prefer not to groove the sides to hold the bottom of the drawer in place, you can instead apply grooved strips of wood to the inside bottom edges of the sides. These are called drawer slips.

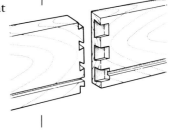

Remember to put the groove where it will be hidden by the dovetails

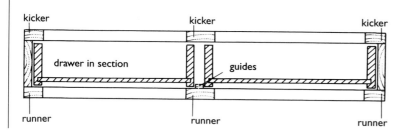

kicker   kicker   kicker

drawer in section   guides

runner   runner   runner

HOW A DRAWER IS SUPPORTED IN A CARCASE

MAKING THE DOVETAIL JOINTS

Lay out and cut the dovetail joints (see page 80) ensuring that the waste is cleaned out from the bottom of each joint. Use half-blind dovetails (see page 82) for the joints at the front of the drawer, but straightforward through dovetails for the two at the back. Always work with the face side and face edge marks in uniform positions – i.e. face side marks pointing inside the drawer and face edge marks facing the bottom.

GLUING THE DRAWER

Make sure that you have cleaned up, sanded and waxed (if you wish) all internal faces before gluing the drawer together. It is very important that when you glue up the drawer, it lies totally flat and is not in any form of twist. When the glue has dried, carefully clean up the dovetails and check the fit of the drawer by first offering the back of the drawer up to the carcase.

On deep drawers, you can put drawer supports underneath to provide extra strength for the bottom. After fitting these, slide the drawer bottom into place. Use birch plywood or better still, for a totally traditional drawer, solid cedar of Lebanon for the bottom. Do not forget that solid wood needs to be able to expand and contract, so do not glue it in place, but screw from underneath into the back of the drawer through slotted holes.

FITTING THE DRAWER

Fit the drawer after cleaning up the dovetails with a smoothing plane (see page 89) and then take off a shaving at a time as needed, checking and rechecking where necessary. If you have waxed the runners, kickers and guides of the carcase before fitting, marks will appear on the drawer showing which areas should be planed off first. After fitting the drawer, lightly sand and wax it (using beeswax or paraffin wax) to help it run smoothly. Drawer stops (not shown on the working drawing) are fitted to the front rail of the cabinet underneath the drawer bottom.

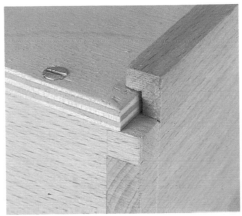

Chamfering the back top edge of the drawer sides prevents air being trapped when the drawer is closed. It also makes it easier to slide the drawer in and out

Underside of drawer: the drawer bottom slides into a groove from the back

DIFFERENT TYPES OF DRAWER

If you wish to create a more decorative drawer, you can adapt it slightly by fitting a cock beading around the drawer front (see opposite). This will make it a little easier to plane and fit into the carcase. Another method is to make a drawer that has a false front, screwing it in place from behind. This will stand proud of the carcase and hide any slight gaps between the drawer and drawer space. In either case it is important to achieve a good fit, as the drawer will either wobble or bind in places if you do not.

You do not necessarily have to make up a drawer using dovetail joints and you may prefer instead to use finger joints or lapped joints which are much easier to make. But for pure strength and decorative effect, a good, well-proportioned dovetail joint wins every time.

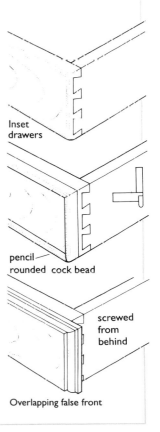

Inset drawers

pencil rounded cock bead

screwed from behind

Overlapping false front

WORKING DRAWINGS

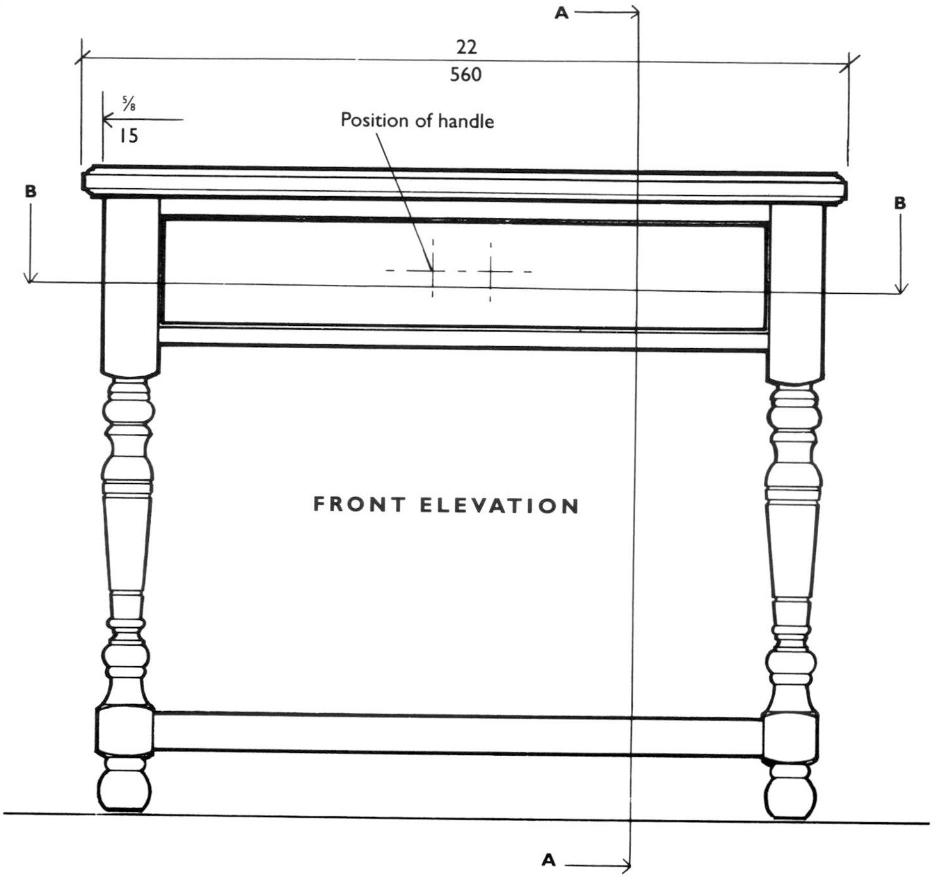
A
22
560
5/8
15
Position of handle
B
B
FRONT ELEVATION
A

DETAIL OF TURNED LEG

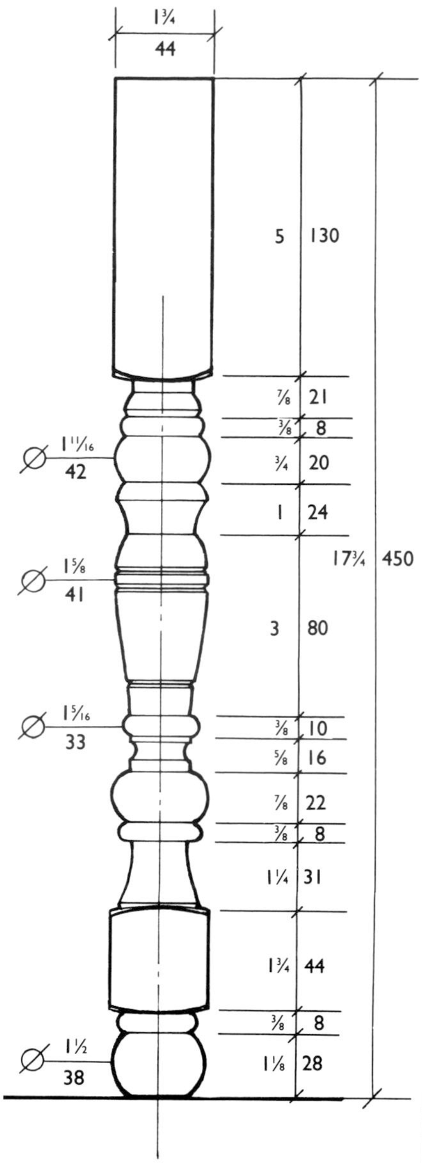
1¾
44
5 | 130
7/8 | 21
3/8 | 8
3/4 | 20
1 | 24
17¾ | 450
3 | 80
3/8 | 10
5/8 | 16
7/8 | 22
3/8 | 8
1¼ | 31
1¾ | 44
3/8 | 8
1⅛ | 28
Ø 1 11/16
42
Ø 1⅝
41
Ø 1 5/16
33
Ø 1½
38

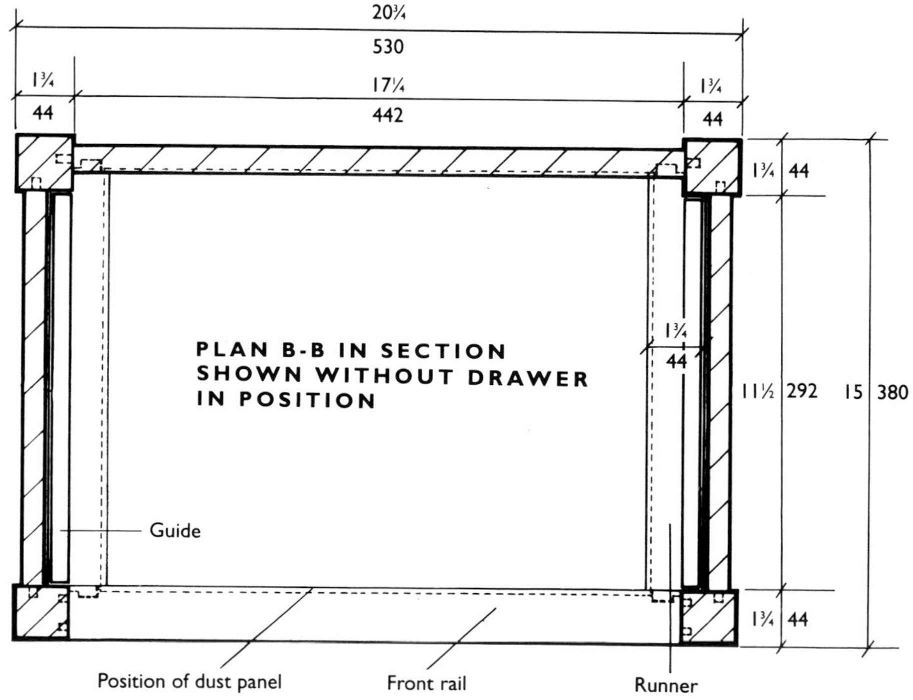
20¾
530
1¾
44
17¼
442
1¾
44
1¾ | 44
1¾
44
11½ | 292
15 | 380
1¾ | 44
PLAN B-B IN SECTION
SHOWN WITHOUT DRAWER
IN POSITION
Guide
Position of dust panel
Front rail
Runner

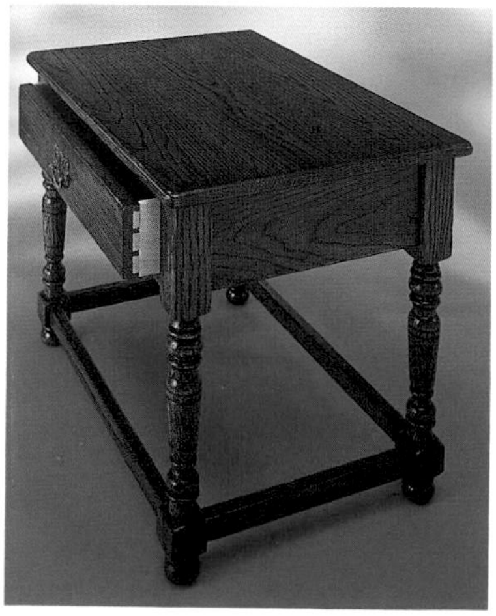

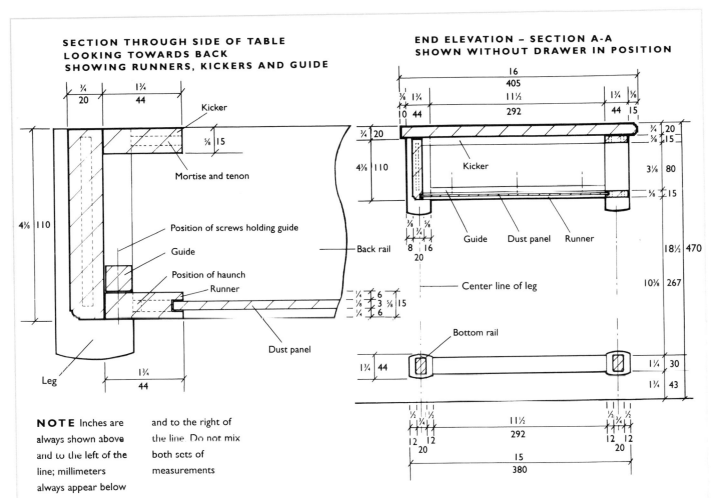

**SECTION THROUGH SIDE OF TABLE
LOOKING TOWARDS BACK
SHOWING RUNNERS, KICKERS AND GUIDE**

**END ELEVATION – SECTION A-A
SHOWN WITHOUT DRAWER IN POSITION**

NOTE Inches are always shown above and to the left of the line; millimeters always appear below and to the right of the line. Do not mix both sets of measurements

CUTTING LIST								
COMPONENT	NUMBER	LENGTH in/mm		WIDTH in/mm		THICKNESS in/mm		COMMENTS
Top	1	22	560	16	405	¾	20	Joined up in 2 pieces
Legs	4	17¾	450	1¾	44	1¾	44	
Bottom rails	2	18¾	480	1¼	30	¾	20	Includes tenons
Bottom rails	2	13	330	1¼	30	¾	20	Includes tenons
Top side rails	2	13	330	4⅜	110	¾	20	Includes tenons
Top back rail	1	18¾	480	4⅜	110	¾	20	Includes tenons
Top front rails	2	18¼	464	1¾	44	⅝	15	Includes tenons
Runners	2	13	330	1¾	44	⅝	15	Includes tenons
Kickers	2	13	330	1¾	44	⅝	15	Includes tenons
Guides	2	11½	292	⅝	16	⅝	16	
Dust panel	1	15½	398	12⅝	320	⅛	3	Birch plywood
Drawer front	1	17¼	442	3⅛	80	¾	20	
Sides	2	11⅜	288	3⅛	80	⅜	9	Beech, oak or maple
Back	1	17¼	442	2⅜	62	⅜	9	Beech, oak or maple
Bottom	1	17	432	11¼	284	¼	6	Birch plywood

Other Books of Interest

Home Construction/Repair
The Art of the Stonemason, $14.95
Gary Branson's Home Repairs and Improvements on a Budget, $16.99
Building & Restoring the Hewn Log House, $18.95
The Complete Guide to Building and Outfitting an Office in Your Home, $18.99
The Complete Guide to Understanding and Caring for Your Home, $18.95
The Complete Guide to Home Automation, $16.95
The Complete Guide to Home Security, $14.95
The Complete Guide to Landscape Design, Renovation, and Maintenance, $14.95
The Complete Guide to Lumber Yards and Home Centers, $5.95
The Complete Guide to Barrier-Free Housing: Convenient Living for the Elderly and the Physically Handicapped, $14.95
The Complete Guide to Decorative Landscaping with Brick and Masonry, $11.95
The Complete Guide to Remodeling Your Basement, $14.95
The Complete Guide to Painting Your Home: Doing it the Way a Professional Does, Inside and Out, $3.95
The Complete Guide to Home Plumbing Repair and Replacement, $16.95
The Complete Guide to Log & Cedar Homes, $16.95
The Complete Guide to Four-Season Home Maintenance: How to Prevent Costly Problems Before They Occur, $18.99
The Complete Guide to Home Roofing Installation and Maintenance, $16.95
The Complete Guide to Manufactured Housing, $14.95
The Complete Guide to Contracting Your Home: A Step-By-Step Guide for Managing Home Construction, 2nd Ed., $18.99
The Complete Guide to Residential Deck Construction, $16.95
Fireplace Designs, $14.95
Get the Most for Your Remodeling Dollar, $7.95
The Home Buyer's Inspection Guide, $12.95
Home Improvements: What Do They Cost, What Are They Worth?, $16.95

Woodworking
The Art of Fine Furniture Building, $16.95
Basic Woodturning Techniques, $14.95
Blizzard's Book of Woodworking, $22.95
Building Fine Furniture From Solid Wood, $24.95
Creating Your Own Woodshop, $18.95
The Complete Guide to Restoring and Maintaining Wood Furniture & Cabinets, $19.95
The Good Wood Handbook, $16.95
Make Your Own Jigs & Woodshop Furniture, $24.99
Make Your Woodworking Pay for Itself, $16.95
Measure Twice, Cut Once, $18.95
Pocket Guide to Wood Finishes, $16.95
Woodworker's Guide to Selecting and Milling Wood, $22.99
The Woodworker's Source Book, $19.95

For a complete catalog of Betterway Books write to the address below. To order, send a check or money order for the price of the book(s). Include $3.00 postage and handling for 1 book, and $1.00 for each additional book. Allow 30 days for delivery.

Betterway Books
1507 Dana Avenue, Cincinnati, Ohio 45207
Credit card orders call TOLL-FREE
1-800-289-0963
Quantities are limited; prices subject to change without notice.

INDEX

Page numbers in *italics* refer to photographs and illustrations

Mark Finney has a background in furniture design and wood technology and a wealth of hands-on practical experience. He owns and runs a furniture making and wood finishing materials business. He teaches courses in all areas of woodworking and writes regularly for *Traditional Woodworking* and *Practical Woodworking* magazines.